ALIEN
ABDUCTION

THE CONTROL FACTOR

JIM BOUCK & ROBERT LONG

Foreword by Kathleen Marden

SCHIFFER
PUBLISHING

4880 Lower Valley Road • Atglen, PA 19310

Type set in Pistolgrip/Nasalization/Roboto

ISBN: 978-0-7643-5966-8
Printed in China

Published by Schiffer Publishing, Ltd.
4880 Lower Valley Road
Atglen, PA 19310
Phone: (610) 593-1777; Fax: (610) 593-2002
E-mail: Info@schifferbooks.com
Web: www.schifferbooks.com

JIM'S DEDICATION

I wish to dedicate this book to my wife, Cathy, for all the support and drive to get me to the finish. To those who have done the research that we've been able to learn from. And, to the brave abductees that have reached out to tell their stories, and given us the information we need to try and solve this phenomenon.

ROBERT'S DEDICATION

I would like to dedicate this book to my wonderful wife, Barb, who stands by my side and smiles as she hears the same UFO story told for the 700th time, and to my two daughters: Samantha, who helped create the book cover from my sketch, and my youngest, Nicole, who always offers her loving support in these endeavors (but secretly thinks Dad is crazy). And finally to my Mom, Thelma, who always encouraged me, never doubted me, and gave me a copy of Whitley Strieber's *Communion* back in 1987, and got this ball rolling.

DON'T BE A VICTIM OR A PAWN; LEARN THE ALIEN ROPES AND THEN RESIST.

CONTENTS

FOREWORD

BY KATHLEEN MARDEN

THE ABDUCTION OF EARTHLINGS BY SPACEFARING ALIENS has aroused public interest since 1966, when *LOOK* magazine ran two feature articles on a New Hampshire couple, Betty and Barney Hill, who claimed to have been abducted by aliens. *The Interrupted Journey*, a full-length book by John G. Fuller, ignited a firestorm of debate on the veracity of memories that had been recovered through hypnosis. Skeptics attributed the story to Betty's dream memories of having been escorted, with her husband, to a disk-shaped craft by small men in blue cadets' attire. Purportedly, these false memories occurred after the Hills thought they had been followed by a bright light in the night sky—a light that instilled terror in Barney, a black man married to a white woman in 1961. Barney's fear of a lynching has been cited as the cause of the trauma that sent him to the office of Boston psychiatrist Benjamin Simon on December 14, 1963, twenty-seven months after the event occurred. What emerged was a startling account of alien abduction.

There is a major problem with the scenario cited above. It completely ignores the evidence that there were at least a dozen witnesses to the UFO, it was picked up on radar, and it hovered within 100 feet of the couple. Barney had conscious recall of observing figures who were dressed in "some type of shiny black uniform" (Betty's September 26, 1961, letter to NICAP) that were "somehow not human" (NICAP investigator Walter Webb's confidential report), the Hills had an inexplicable two-hour time loss, and there was startling circumstantial and physical evidence. The incident, the documented evidence, and the cover-up are presented in my seminal book, with nuclear physicist Stanton Friedman, in *Captured! The Betty and Barney Hill UFO Experience.*

A dramatic two-hour motion picture, *The UFO Incident*, starring James Earl Jones and Estelle Parsons, added fuel to the fire in the minds of the American public when it aired on October 20, 1975. The Hills and a long trail of subsequent abductees were subjected to oppressive scrutiny by self-styled skeptics who used speculation and disinformation to twist the events and destroy the reputations of people whose lives had already been traumatically disrupted. One disinformant became the "go to" guy for the mainstream media and joyfully disparaged ordinary people who had become victims of alien abduction when their stories of compelling evidence were made public, sometimes without their consent. (See my book with Stanton Friedman, *Fact, Fiction, and Flying Saucers*, for additional information.)

Jim Bouck and Bob Long, in this fascinating book, present a well-documented overview of the early pioneers of abduction research. Most notably, Budd Hopkins went to the aid of abductees who were suffering trauma and anxiety related to their incomplete memories of abduction and missing time. He conducted groundbreaking research on alien abduction with hundreds of individuals and offered hypnosis and support groups for the victims. In response to this, self-styled skeptics attempted to destroy his reputation and findings, casting abductees as the dupes of Budd Hopkins.

David Jacobs, an assistant professor of history at Temple University, published his first book, *The UFO Controversy in America*, in 1975. He took on the psychologists who proclaimed abduction was the result of mass hysteria, collective hallucinations, and public suggestibility and demolished the credibility of the US Air Force's proclamation that UFOs exhibited characteristics in keeping with our technological development. He made it clear that the CIA had instigated the debunking of UFO reports and stood in the way of congressional inquiry and the scientific investigation of the UFO presence.

The authors explore the seminal work of John Mack, MD, a distinguished psychiatrist at Harvard University who conducted hundreds of hours of interviews and treatment with abduction experiencers who had undergone profound psychological and spiritual conversions. Their stories challenged our fundamental understanding of mankind's place in the universe. As a consequence of his courageous scientific exploration, his colleagues attempted to have him censured. But in the face of the zeitgeist of the old guard, Dr. Mack ultimately prevailed.

Whereas Hopkins and Jacobs took a dim view of extraterrestrial (ET) abduction, Mack acknowledged the complexity of contact and its transformative power. These transformations have been studied and confirmed by academic researchers.

It was Mack's intellectual curiosity and courage that propelled me into the field of research on experiencers of UFO contact. I sought the assistance of a fearless academic, Don C. Donderi, PhD, a retired associate professor of psychology at McGill University and associate dean of the faculty of graduate studies and research. He had worked on an alien symbols study in association with Budd Hopkins and on the development of the American Personality Inventory (API) with psychiatric social worker Ted Davis and Hopkins. The API was developed to assess the truth of whether someone had been abducted by extraterrestrials.

Dr. Donderi and I have recently collaborated on a three-year comprehensive research study on 516 experiencers of ET contact. Most participants were referred to our study by members of MUFON's experiencer research team (ERT), of which I am the director. ERT members Craig Lang, MS (1956–2018); Michael Austin Melton, PhD; Denise Stoner; and I developed a 118-question survey exclusively for people who believed they had been contacted or abducted by ETs. Our objective was to identify a variety of characteristics that experiencers share and to collect statistical data that would be of value to MUFON investigators, researchers, and experiencers alike. Our questions were straightforward and pertained to the abduction/contact experience, based upon our investigative findings, the historical discoveries of other researchers, the psychological research findings in a variety of academic studies, and the postulates offered by prominent skeptics. The survey questions pertained to demographics, family structure, generational contact, religious/spiritual beliefs, emotional impact, medical impact, psychic and paranormal phenomena, perceived treatment by ETs, descriptions of the nonhuman intelligent entities, the contact experience, MILABS, and the messages they received.

Dr. Donderi administered the API to the 175 of the 516 participants who agreed to participate in phase 2 of our study. He discovered that all of the 175 phase 2 participants were distributed along a wide range in reference to the "Abductee" target—those who had all of the characteristics of "alien abduction syndrome." Many scored at the Abductee target, and no one fell into the Control (general population) or Simulator (wannabe) groups. This gave us insight into the characteristics exhibited by UFO abductees versus the groups who reported highly positive and negative experiences. We discovered that the majority of UFO abductees had recurring events throughout their lifetime. They reported intergenerational contact, increased psychic ability (including the psychic condition of being empathic), increased paranormal activity such as light orbs, and increased spirituality. They had been taken from their beds but were awake and moving before paralysis set in. Many believe that they have been healed of a physical condition by their ET visitors. Their attitude toward contact was determined by the type of entity they encountered. Some are more benevolent than others. When asked if they would end contact today if it were possible, 75 percent of the UFO abductees chose to continue contact despite the sometimes frightening, even traumatic emotional impact.

Bouck and Long address much of this information in their fascinating book, and more. They tackle scientific discoveries on the nature of memory. Why do some memories remain clear in our minds despite the passage of time, when others are fleeting? Why do abductees forget their interactions with the ETs who have taken them into an alien environment? Why can hypnosis recover lost memories? How can we know that recovered memories are real?

The authors push beyond the human factors to the exploration of theoretical physics. Can physics explain why ETs seem to possess the scientific knowledge to quickly traverse the galaxy? Is it possible for a body to survive the g-force of highly advanced craft that violate our laws of physics? Why do their aerial vehicles seem to simply disappear or instantaneously phase in or out? Why do ETs appear to be interdimensional and metaphysical? How can they move an abductee through a solid surface such as a closed window or the roof of a building?

Without a doubt, you will enjoy this well-written, fascinating book, which attempts to answer these questions: "Who are these ETs? What are they doing here? And what is the science that makes these events happen?"

—Kathleen Marden
UFO and abduction/contact researcher, author, and lecturer
MUFON director of Experiencer Research
Edgar Mitchell Foundation for Research into Extraterrestrial and
Extraordinary Encounters Board of Directors member

INTRODUCTION

SINCE THE LATE 1940S, HUMANS HAVE BEEN captivated by sightings of strange and unexplainable unidentified flying objects (UFOs). UFOs have interacted with our military aircraft for decades in cat-and-mouse games. The story of Betty and Barney Hill, a couple abducted on their return home from a vacation trip in New Hampshire in September 1961, captivated people as the story made major news and the cover of *LOOK* magazine. In the mid-eighties, many books hit the shelves, written by researchers working with people claiming stories of being abducted by strange alien creatures. These stories suggested that US citizens as well as others from around the world were being taken aboard UFOs for bizarre medical procedures, totally against their will. The US military, meanwhile, always did their best to pooh-pooh the whole phenomenon in public while trying their best to glean any information about UFO capabilities and technology that they could.

Who is truly looking for answers? If we, as a race, take a hundred years to solve a puzzle, in some respects it's sort of like trying not to solve anything at all. The numbers say we should be trying harder.

In 1991, a Roper poll was commissioned dealing specifically with the alien abduction phenomenon, and the results suggested the possibility that as many as four million people in the US (at that time) had and were having their lives altered by secretive abduction experiences involving strange creatures from places other than here—the effects of these experiences were being felt physically and psychologically. People having these strange experiences began showing signs of post-traumatic stress disorder (PTSD). The phenomenon was becoming a serious life-altering event, and those involved were looking for help.

We recall one woman who contacted us for help. She told her story to us, at least what she could remember from bits and pieces that were coming back to her. In a matter of a day she suddenly decided to check herself into a psychiatric hospital. When we asked why she had done this, she replied that it was better to believe that she had experienced some type of psychological breakdown than to believe that what she was remembering were things that had happened to her. To her, crazy was a more comforting choice.

So, where are we now? What have we learned? Through anecdotal testimony, we have learned about sixty-eight years of hide and seek with UFOs and their occupants. We are going to take a look at how these reported experiences, and the entities that have been able to engineer them, have altered the lives of certain individuals. We will show how control is taken from these people. How pieces of their own body's tissue are removed without their consent. They are poked and prodded, sometimes feeling excruciating pain. These are everyday people subjected to mental manipulation to make them do things against their will, with no personal control.

For example: A man and his wife were driving along a major highway when they noticed what appeared to be an unidentified flying object fly across their view and appear to land on the other side of the road, just out of sight. The husband quickly pulled over to the side of the road, near an overpass bridge abutment. Heart pounding, he grabbed his camera and told his wife he was going to climb up the abutment and onto the bridge, cross to the other side, and take pictures of the UFO. He grabbed the door handle and was all set to go when suddenly he hesitated. He froze for a few seconds as if processing what he was about to do, when, unexpectedly, he returned the camera to the back seat. He looked forward, put the car in gear, and proceeded to drive off down the road as before the sighting.

His wife, somewhat puzzled, asked why he wasn't going after this once-in-a-lifetime photograph. He said that he just didn't think it would be worth it. He said that by the time he got up the hill to cross the bridge, the UFO would have been gone, and it just wasn't worth it. A few miles down the road, the husband suddenly realized what had just transpired, becoming upset and extremely bewildered with his recent behavior. He now wanted to take the picture, but of course it was too late. They were miles down the road from where the sighting had occurred.

What happened? This is what is believed to be an insidious manipulation of the human psyche by an outside force. Abduction researchers see this type of scenario again and again. It is common among the testimonial anecdotes we hear. Did the husband really think that it would be gone, or was he made to think that, just to discourage him from taking the picture?

Sometimes, some people are made to do things they don't want to do or are manipulated not to do something they want to do. Why and how is this possible? This might have been a chance in a lifetime to photograph a UFO, and as excited as the hubby was to take the picture, he seemed to suddenly and unexplainably just lose interest.

This book will deal with situations like these, and others, where it seems as if the person was controlled to alter his excitement and his actions to suit that of another's command. How would it be possible in this example, since his wife was the only one with the man in the car, and she wanted the photo as much as he did? We hope to discover and explain how he was able to be controlled and who controlled him.

We will be looking at lots of firsthand testimony, cutting-edge scientific theory, and quantum mechanics to explain in real-life terms how this could happen. It's not magic or mystic. The magician pulls a rabbit out of a hat or pretends to cut a woman in two, but it is just mechanics, psychology, and useful misdirection. So it's not magic. UFOs and their pilots aren't magical either. They're just better at the science than we are.

Control like this has been reported by many people in circumstances involving a close encounter or where an alien abduction was about to take place. Alien interference seems to be involved, but how did they do it? To find a solution to this problem we need to learn about how people can be controlled. How is it that a man or woman supposedly in full control of his or her actions can relinquish such control? What is control in general, and how can it be used? Do alien creatures have the technology to exert their will on us when it suits their need? Let's take a look at control in our everyday lives, and how it not only affects us, but how we strive to achieve it.

01

WHAT IS CONTROL?

FROM THE SECOND WE ARE BORN, WE learn about our environment and find ways of trying to control it. The infant learns to cry to illicit a response from its mother, thereby engaging its first attempt at control of being fed or changed or held. A parent who comes rushing every time an infant cries is handing the keys of control over to the child, who learns that a cry is a method of bringing about the meeting of its needs. The child has learned its first form of control on its environment. We do not mean to sound cold, mechanical, or without a bond of love here; we're just looking at the basics of survival of a newest member of our species.

At preschool, a child learns that other children have found methods of control as well, but this control will spill over into conflicts—maybe over a toy or for attention. It may be playful control or forceful or even confrontational in nature. We believe that some children learn to manipulate other children at a very early age—a bully in the making, perhaps, brought about by the need to feel in control at school because the feeling of control may not be present at home. The need to feel in some type of control comes early to us.

Grade school steps up the control need to another level. Any parent will tell you that once their child reaches grade school, they change—and not always for the better. Issues arise at school with societal pressures from classmates that bleed over to the home. Mom and Dad are now slowly becoming the ruling class, and the child develops the need for independence.

The need for the child's wishes of unbridled control is about to bring an end to paradise for the parents, who now start to develop their own feelings of diminishing control as the child progresses socially.

From there it is just a blur for the ever-growing need to control one's life. The high school student is testing the controls laid down by dear old mom and dad. Testing boundaries that have been set forth over the years and have gone unquestioned are now seemingly always up for review by the budding teenager. Somehow the child has become a Supreme Court judge questioning the constitutionality of a parent's every rule. The end is near as every parent feels their loving, nurturing, parenting control start to slip through their fingers as the child becomes an adult—a natural process, we might add, and one we all reflect on in a positive way . . . hopefully.

College: This is often the first time that the newly emerging adult has been given the keys of control to take for a test drive, sent off to college, often in another state, hundreds of miles from the control of mom and dad. No curfew, no oversight; all rules are up for interpretation. *Wahoo*, spring break; let's open this baby up and see what she will do! Control gone wild. Sometimes our first taste of unbridled control does not go as well as originally planned, and we learn to throttle it back a little, sometimes with the help of law enforcement—hopefully, setting a baseline for a little self-control lesson.

Sometimes self-control needs a little help. This is why we have laws controlling the amount of alcohol you can have in your body's bloodstream, or the type of drugs you can take that might inhibit your level of self-control and make you a danger to yourself and others.

How much control is enough? That depends on who you are when it comes to personality. Perhaps you are what the public commonly perceives as the typical type "A" personality, and you really need to feel in control or, worse, fear that everything will come crashing down if you are not. Perhaps the thought of not being in control will keep you up at night and supply a therapist with steady income for a while. The point that we are trying to make here is that all of us wish to have as much control and freedom in our lives as we can. Some strive to have higher levels of control than others, and some take it to extremes.

What doesn't help is that it seems that everyone else we have any contact with wants to control us in a variety of ways, as we do to them. Our circle of influence is intertwined with a number of other people, each with their own circle. We might feel that we are controlled by our spouse, or our boss, our government, our income, our race, our age, our level of education, on and on and on. It may be perceived or factual, but it is there, our need for control.

How many of you out there in the last couple of years have found that someone else controlled your job, and you were suddenly unemployed? Now lack of finances severely chisels away at your grasp on control. In fact, the average person tends to dislike those who have wealth, because with wealth comes a higher degree of power and control. Just one more person above us on the chain of control. Frustrating, isn't it?

We all want it. We all strive to have it—or the illusion of it. We all fool ourselves, secretly knowing we are not really at the helm. The one thing that keeps us from going insane with all of this is the fact that we know all the players who have some control of our lives. For example: government entities like the IRS, or a utility company, that if we don't pay our bill, the lights or phone may go dead. Or even our boss, who may crack the whip of control over our heads to drive us to conform or to excel.

Knowing whom we must appease (e.g., pay the power company or the IRS) to maintain our level of personal control over our lives is what keeps us going. Everyone has their own list of whom they must pay or appease to be happy and ultimately survive.

As adults, we continue to seek our precious control. In fact, it never stops. We seek to control relationships with spouses, children, our friends, maybe even our pets, who at times have issues with our desire for control at the supper table. We wish to control our job, our property, our destiny, when in reality, all we can truly control is ourselves, our thoughts, and reactions to what happens in our daily lives, and within our personal internal control.

On a larger scale, some countries strive to control religions, borders, or natural resources. Take a country like Israel having to wrestle to control their borders against an impending crush from others states who wish to control the Holy Lands and deny the Jews their religion and existence. Others wish to control the oil flow and thus have the power to affect economies. The first Iraq war came about when Saddam Hussein attacked Kuwait, including their rich oil fields. That was when the United States stepped in with their form of control and militarily pushed Hussein's forces out of Kuwait.

At this point we would like to make one thing very clear. Not all control is bad, and in fact it is critically needed. A toddler must be controlled for their own safety. A teenager . . . just goes without saying. A state must control the populace with laws to protect personal life, liberty, and the pursuit of happiness. A car, plane, train, or human being out of control can be a dangerous thing. The point we are trying to make is that control is a very intimate part of our being.

What this book is about is control of another form, not human in nature, but that we are being defiled and controlled by nonhuman creatures from somewhere other than here. They are breaking the laws of our land and insulting us as sentient beings through psychological manipulation, treating us like cattle. (And we certainly don't treat cattle very well in most places here on Earth. This topic would be a whole different book.) This book is about the misdeeds reportedly done to human beings, the means by which these things are done to us, and how we may affect or regain this control of this outside manipulation by entities not of our world.

Definition:

The Merriam-Webster online dictionary says that control is to exercise restraining or directing influence over, regulate, have power over, rule, or reduce the incidence or severity of, especially to innocuous levels (e.g., *control* an insect population or *control* a disease). [We've seen enough sci-fi movies where some alien species considered *us* the disease.]

One means of gaining control over someone is with physical force. The stronger or smarter someone is, the more control he or she may have on a subject. Another means to control is to make the subject want to be controlled or to think that it is natural to do the bidding of the one in control. Physical force is easy to explain and to understand, but to make one be controlled willingly, not just through the use of physical control but also by thought process and decision making, is necessary.

What is mind control? When one thinks of mind control, one might automatically think of cartoons where the mad, crazy hypnotist mesmerizes his subject and makes him do things that would never be done by a sane and conscious person. Another thought would be the stage hypnotist who makes his subject bark like a dog on a given signal or jump at the clap of hands.

Yet, a couple more examples of mind control in a much more insidious way would be the Reverend Jim Jones and the Heaven's Gate cults. Jones was the founder and leader of the Peoples Temple, which is best known for the November 18, 1978, mass suicide of 909 temple members in Jonestown, Guyana. The Heaven's Gate cult was a religious group based in San Diego, California, founded and led by Marshall Applewhite. On March 26, 1997, police discovered the bodies of thirty-nine members of the group who had committed suicide, including Applewhite—in order to reach what they believed was an alleged alien spacecraft that was supposed to be following the comet Hale-Bopp, which was at its brightest in the evening sky at the time.

But, true mind control is not induced by hypnotists, and even the greatest hypnotist cannot hypnotize someone into doing something that the person does not consciously want to do. Stage hypnotists search the crowd for people of high suggestibility, knowing that they will be better subjects to choose for a good show. In other words, the inclination must be there. You probably would not be able to make a person who would never commit murder do so, but hypnotizing a convicted murderer to do it again might not be such a stretch.

History is full of attempts to control others. Imagine if it were possible to be able to control one or more people at a time. Certain countries would kill for that type of control. That may sound harsh, but certain governments have done more for less. With that type of power and control, one country could dominate another without ever firing a bullet or missile. All they would have to do is push the proverbial button, tell the other's army to surrender, and remove the head of the government by simply giving an order. The entire world would be a potential slave to whoever could enact this type of control.

02

THE ART OF ABDUCTION

BY DEFINITION, ABDUCTION IS WHEN A MAN, woman, or child is taken from his or her environment without their consent, or the consent of a supervising adult. We consider this to be kidnapping. Kidnapping, of course, is a federal offense in the United States. Traveling tourists in certain Third World countries have become targets to kidnappers on a regular basis. Tourists being held for a ransom and not freed until it is paid is becoming a serious travel problem. Some people now hire bodyguards while on vacation. Trafficking in human slavery especially with women and children is becoming more common in the news.

What happens when one is kidnapped can be very traumatic and extremely dangerous. These are often life-threatening circumstances to the person who has been taken. The family and friends of the kidnapped victim panic and do whatever they can to bring the person back safely. The police and FBI will usually get involved and also do whatever they can to bring the victim back safely and catch the perpetrators of the crime. After all, we are talking about a crime in all fifty states in the US and most all other civilized countries as well. When returned, if returned at all, the victim will usually be sent to a hospital for an examination to determine if he or she had been sexually assaulted or harmed in any physical way. The psychological trauma from a kidnapping event may last a lifetime.

The testimony of that victim is accepted almost without question. The accused is almost always presumed guilty until proven innocent. The abduction of this victim can cause a drastic change in the life of that individual and their family. What the kidnapper did was illegal and just plain wrong, in any region or culture on this planet. The abductor, if caught, will be prosecuted and punished—in some countries by death. If not caught, the perpetrator will be pursued until brought to justice. A point we would like to make here is that if it is a severe enough crime, the law enforcement personnel on the case do not give up either until the perpetrator of the crime is caught or no shred of evidence can be found to pursue the case any further.

Now, let's look at another kind of kidnapping. A crime that remains hidden and hushed up. The victim of the crime is ridiculed and disbelieved, called the perpetrator of a hoax, or labeled as mentally imbalanced or just someone who seeks attention. We've heard all kinds of unkind things said about people who are claiming to have experienced an abduction event by some type of unexplainable creature to a place that seems to be aboard a craft not of this world.

THE TOPIC OF ALIEN ABDUCTION

This kind of kidnapping may occur while you are in your home or in a car and driving down the road, or from anywhere you, the victim, happens to be at the time. One reason that not much is done for the victim is that the person taken often never realizes that it happened at the time of the event, with beginning event memories of seeing a strange light in the sky and ending event memories of seeing it fly away. Often unnoticed is a period of missing time that has happened between those two memory fragments. Bits and pieces of memory pertaining to the event may come back over time as disjointed flashbacks and manifest itself as post-traumatic stress symptoms. Often, family and friends present at the abduction event have been "turned off" or put into some type of a frozen state of animation; if they are not being taken, they may be unaware of the event, except for an uncomfortable void of time that they all share and perhaps a sighting of something strange in the sky. Because of this, the victim is almost always alone in fear and frustration. Shared events are rarely talked about, as if those present were in some way told not to do so.

The victim, who is always returned (we say always because if they were not, we would never know, and they would just become a missing person), may not recall any of the events during the time away or even know there was a kidnapping. Abductees, whose memory of being taken is completely wiped out, face the same initial shock and terror every time it happens, as if it was their first time. We personally believe this is cruel. Never remembering, never lessening the fear. In one sense, people who have been through a hypnotic regression and may be able to piece some of their memories together can usually deal or cope with some of the fear. They are still scared, but at least they now realize what is going on and can prepare themselves better. The family and friends may never know, and if they do, they may go into denial and ridicule the victim or tell him or her to keep quiet about it or people will think that he or she is crazy. The police and FBI will definitely never get involved, and there will never be a pursuit of the abductor. The government has done almost everything it could do to make everybody think that if they see a UFO, let alone experience abduction, they are misidentifying what they saw, or they are trying to perpetrate a hoax, or they are just plainly psychotic.

The reason for this discrepancy in action is because of the skeptical nature to those ignorant of the facts—or fear of belief. The abductor in our everyday world is always either a man or woman (or both)—textbook and normal by all standards for law enforcement. The abductor in the latter situation is a life form from somewhere else, presumed not to be Earth. This is something that is just too unimaginable to mention, something to be scoffed at as drug-induced imagination or a mental aberration and not taken seriously. If an abductee recalls the events, it is quite often fragmented and disjointed—very frightening and even *too* frightening to describe. They can't believe it themselves, so how could they logically expect anyone else to believe it? It stays packed inside and begins to fester.

They may recall, again—if they recall at all—being taken from their bed at night, or from their car, or the beach, store, train, or anywhere. There seems to be no limits to when and where a victim can be snatched. The victim is not always taken when sleeping. A lot of them are wide awake and may even be in the company of others. Some have been taken from small groups or even abducted within a small group, such as the Allagash Abductions. This documented case of multiple alien abduction, which occurred in August 1976 in the state of Maine, gained worldwide attention when it was dramatized in an episode of television's *Unsolved Mysteries*. Twin brothers Jack and Jim Weiner, along with their friends, Chuck Rak and Charlie Foltz, would be unwilling participants in a UFO sighting, possibly a period of missing time, and some of them remember an Abduction event.

They all were art students, having met at the Massachusetts College of Art. What should have been a relaxing fishing trip was anything but. The four of them had canoed to Eagle Lake. They decided to do a little night fishing and built a roaring fire at their camp on the bank to use as a landmark so they wouldn't lose their way back in the dark.

After a short period of time, all four of the men's attention was drawn to a large, bright light in the sky over the lake. It was *very* bright. It appeared to be only a couple of hundred yards away, hovering over a grouping of trees. The object began to move and change color. The men estimated it to be about 80 feet in diameter. Charlie Foltz decided to signal to it with his flashlight. (Never a good idea.) All at once, it began to move toward them.

The UFO silently moved in their direction. They began to paddle wildly for the shoreline, going as fast as they could. A light beam from the object came down and engulfed them and their canoe. The next thing they knew, they were back at camp on the shore. Foltz again tried to signal the UFO with his flashlight (Charlie not remembering that this did not turn out so well the first time)—but this time it shot upward and took off. The guys noticed that the large fire they had started as a signal fire that they could see out on the lake to relocate their camp after fishing—seemingly only a short time ago—was already burned to ashes. It didn't seem like that much time had passed. What had happened to them?

We've seen the hoaxers, the imbalanced, and the attention seekers. We have talked with the ones who thought it would be a great joke to play on investigators to make claims of alien abduction. We've seen people who drink too much and see little green men, and then we have seen just everyday people who drink too much, *because* they have seen little Grey ones.

03

TALL TALES THROUGHOUT HISTORY?

HISTORY IS FULL OF SOMETIMES COLORFUL STORIES about people being taken and kept or held against their will by aliens. Some of these stories when told are easily accepted as a kind of fabrication, often with the blame given to flights of fancy or overconsumption of some alcoholic brew. The book *Passport to Magonia: From Folklore to Flying Saucers*, written by Jacques Vallée in 1969, is loaded with anecdotes about people of many cultures having contact with "little people." Over centuries, these little people have been given names like elves, leprechauns, angels, sprites, demons, and faeries—cross-cultural stories of small creatures from other worlds or underworlds that seem to possess "powers" of control over the common man. The book is about visitors from other worlds, and yes, we do mean extraterrestrials, and while the little-people stories are superficially different, there are fundamental similarities with modern-day abduction stories.

"Rip Van Winkle" is a story written by Washington Irving about a man who lived in the Catskill Mountains of New York State. One day, Rip Van Winkle decided to leave his farm to escape a day's work and the nagging of his wife. He went into the mountains to do some hunting with his dog. Rip heard a voice calling out his name, and, looking for the source, he found a short little man who enticed Rip to follow him farther into the mountains. There he saw more people going about their business. Rip helped the short man set down a keg of liquor that they had carried up to a place in the mountains. Rip took a drink from the keg and became sleepy. When he finally awoke from his sleep, he headed back to town only to discover that he had been away for twenty years, and everything had changed. As he told his story of seeing this person and going to the mountainous location, most people listened with smirks and disbelief.

And then there is the childhood story of "The Pied Piper." This was a story about a town that had been overrun by rats. The rats were everywhere, and the people pleaded with the town leaders to do something to get rid of all the creatures. The leaders tried various ways to rid the town of the rodents, but nothing worked. One day a man with a flute came into town claiming he could get rid of them for a large fee. The town leaders did not want to pay the fee but were at wits end—so they agreed. The piper began to play his instrument, and all the rats in the town followed him out of the town. When the piper went back to get his pay, the town leaders refused to pay him. He gave them a warning that if they did not pay, they would regret it. No payment was made, and none was going to be made, so the piper once again played his instrument. This time all the children of the town followed him out of the town and were never seen again.

We are not suggesting for a second that these stories are based on anything but fantasy. They are simply childhood stories about people being taken and some form of control being used on them. We can't say that we would write a child's story and include abduction, but perhaps times have changed, as they say.

Aliens in Our Mainstream Society: Movie and TV Shows

Aliens, whether fictional ones or actual living entities, have worked their way into our everyday lives: Their likenesses are on bumper stickers with funny sayings, on candy containers, on road signs, and in TV commercials. They sell cars, drink beer, and bring dead birds back to life before eating them while on a trek to escape Area 51 in the movie *Paul*. *Paul* was a humorous 2011 British American science fiction comedy film directed by Greg Mottola, written by Simon Pegg and Nick Frost. The public loved "Mork from Ork" of the *Mork & Mindy* television show, which was an American sci-fi sitcom broadcast on the ABC network from 1978 until 1982. Mork was a hilarious, friendly, and misunderstood space alien trying to understand human ways, played by the late world-famous comedian and actor Robin Williams (1951–2014), who may, after all, have been a space alien. (Just kidding.) Parting thought here, if you woke up in your room in the middle of the night, paralyzed, with a strange light coming in the window, and saw Robin Williams standing there, how would you react? Even starting as early as 1963 with the TV show *My Favorite Martian*, played by Ray Walston, who portrayed a marooned Martian on Planet Earth. During his stay, he portrayed the part of Bill Bixby's Uncle Martin as he tried to learn the ways of Earth. We enjoy humor and employ it where we can, especially to lighten up such a serious topic, just as has been done with the above-mentioned shows and movies—a friendly face to alien contact may be a pleasant thing. We would like nothing better than to have an intelligent, benevolent, extraterrestrial race contact us and show us ways to better our world with free clean energy and unlimited food, and to show us the way to enlightenment, if you will. That may be nice . . . but may not be realistic.

Stephen Hawking: Alien Contact Could Be Risky

In a Discovery Channel documentary that aired in April 2010, British astrophysicist Stephen Hawking (1942—2018) said that communicating with aliens could be a threat to Earth. Hawking said it is likely that alien life exists (some of us agree with that more than others), but a visit from extraterrestrials might be similar to Christopher Columbus's arrival in the New World.

"If aliens visit us, the outcome would be much as when Columbus landed in America, which didn't turn out well for the Native Americans," Hawking said. "We only have to look at ourselves to see how intelligent life might develop into something we wouldn't want to meet."

In the program, *Into the Universe with Stephen Hawking*, he speculated that alien capabilities "would be only limited by how much power they could harness and control, and that could be far more than we might first imagine." He said it might even be possible for aliens to harvest the energy from an entire star. "Such advanced aliens would perhaps become nomads, looking to conquer and colonize whatever planets they can reach" (*ABC News*, April 26, 2010).

We, personally, are going to stop and listen to someone who was perhaps, arguably, the greatest mind of our time since Albert Einstein. Maybe the SETI program wasn't such a hot idea after all.

Movie Monsters

In many cases, aliens are a product of our imagination. The movie aliens have thrilled us . . . and scared us to death. In the *Alien* movie series, which starred Sigourney Weaver, Swiss artist H. R. Giger achieved international fame with his work on Ridley Scott's *Alien* franchise, consisting of six movies to date. We like the adrenalin rush of make-believe monsters. We spend millions of dollars seeing them on the silver screen. In a way, we do crave the thrill and the threat, hoping to never really meet a monster.

Interestingly enough, no one has ever come forward claiming to have seen one of H. R. Giger's creations—or any other movie monster—in their bedroom, trying to abduct them. With all the horrible and hideous aliens that our imaginations have created on the big screen and TV, they never show up in stories reported by people claiming to be abducted. If these people were weak-minded, fantasy-prone individuals as some debunkers suggest, our imaginary aliens should be expected to leak into the dreams of these people who supposedly can't tell the difference between a dream and reality. That doesn't seem to happen.

On the other side, not until well after abduction stories started to surface in the sixties did we see anything resembling the little Grey aliens in movie media or TV. The first two that come to mind are the Travis Walton abduction in Arizona back in 1975. *Fire in the Sky* was a 1993 horror-based science fiction movie about an alleged extraterrestrial encounter, directed by Robert Lieberman and written by Tracy Tormé (his father was noted singer Mel Tormé), which was based somewhat loosely, I might add, on Travis Walton's book *The Walton Experience*. Travis wanted the story to be factual; Tormé wanted to sell the story to Hollywood and knew that if it was to work, it would have to be tweaked to get them to bite. Travis needed to get the true story out, and he suffered frustration over the creative license Hollywood used to sell and promote it. We hope the public never used the "true story" aspect of the Hollywood version of the movie as a gauge for abduction or of Walton himself. Abductees never report waking up on a craft encased in a cubicle of slimy goo.

The second modern alien abduction TV miniseries was *Taken*, also known as *Steven Spielberg Presents Taken*, which was a science fiction miniseries that first aired on the Sci-Fi Channel in 2002 and won an Emmy Award for Outstanding Miniseries. The story was written by Leslie Bohem, and the executive producers were Bohem and Steven Spielberg.

The story line takes place from 1944 to 2002 and follows the lives of three families, all of whom have direct contact with the typical Grey aliens. While creative license is always present, they covered the Roswell crash and cover-up, abductions, implants, and the breeding program to ultimately create a hybrid species. Reception was positive, and the series won an Emmy.

LITTLE GREEN MEN

The whole "little green men from Mars" thing didn't even bleed over into abduction stories. You see little green Martians in cartoons, again in bumper stickers, and in assorted merchandising ads, but we have never had a case reported where an abductee said that their captors were green in color—where again, if they were these weak-minded individuals, they should have, to add credibility to their supposedly contrived stories.

It is almost like a friendly face has been painted on the human abductors, either to keep the abduction as a joke or make it into one. Why? Is it joking about the 800-pound gorilla in the room that no one wants to take seriously or be faced with a severe change to our worldview? Is it a plan for indoctrinating them into our society and to keep people from taking a threat seriously? Is it an initiation of mind control? Is it an insidious effort to dig its tendril into our lives?

Years ago, a man we consider a friend and colleague, David M. Jacobs, PhD, an American historian and recently retired associate professor of history at Temple University specializing in twentieth-century American history and culture, wrote *The UFO Controversy in America*. (Bloomington: Indiana University Press, 1975). He became interested in the stories of alien abduction and how they were affecting our culture. In 1992, he wrote *Secret Life: Firsthand Accounts of UFO Abductions* (New York: Simon & Schuster, 1992). Jacobs became an expert on the subject of alien abduction. His third book, *The Threat: Revealing the Secret Alien Agenda* (New York: Simon & Schuster, 1998), was where it began to hit the fan, as they say. We recall Dave talking about all the hate mail he got over the content of that book. Being a historian, Dave took all the information that was available about alien abduction and started assembling a chronological record of the events pertaining to the topic, giving it a historical perspective. Of particular interest was the escalation of events. Abduction stories of bigger craft, more crew, more exam tables, and multiple abductees at one time suggested that the project was picking up pace. It painted a very dark picture of alien abduction and implied it was going to lead to the demise of the human race.

We thought it was a great read and had a logical progression that only a historian could present. It made sense. We personally hoped like hell that he was wrong, but were very concerned that he was not. Jacobs himself said he hoped he was wrong. He got blasted over writing the book. He had crossed some imaginary line in the hearts and minds of some of the abductees. Many fired back at him, stating that he must be wrong for being so blunt and stating that this was an ongoing invasion. Many felt he had gone way overboard. We thought he was courageous for doing what he felt he had to do. The facts as he knew them pointed to a logical conclusion. After all, historians do know something about invasions! If he turned out to be wrong, then great. If he turned out to be right, then oh crap! We need to take some of the hypotheses in this book and find some answers, turn them into theories, and produce countermeasures—sooner rather than later.

As we mentioned earlier, what if a force could take over without bloodshed? Without firing a shot? What if you could gain control over your adversary and not even have your opponent know? Wouldn't that be a better way to take over than the ways we have concocted over the past few millennia? Death, destruction, and ruin have been, and are, our way. We're beginning to see why the peaceful aliens haven't landed. Or maybe they did and we shot them, like in the movie *The Day the World Stood Still* (1951). It would be just like us to accidentally shoot the wrong ones.

Sun Tzu wrote the *Art of War*. It is still taught today at the War College, which is an educational institution in Carlisle, Pennsylvania. Sun Tzu was into controlling his opponent—and controlling the battlefield. He wrote that war is based on deception. It is a doctrine of war that we must not rely on the likelihood of the enemy not coming, but on our readiness to meet him; not on the chance of his not attacking, but on the fact that we have made our position invincible (from a translation of the *Art of War*, Sun Tzu, 500 BCE).

DEBUNKING THE THREAT

For something that some debunkers say does not exist, these alien abduction stories sure do show up in our culture a lot. Some debunkers might say that all the abduction phenomenon is a subconscious wish to be scared, or to be thrilled, or to gain attention—that it is a psychological issue or that it is partially physiological due to dream state paralysis, or altered states of consciousness such as the hypnopompic or hypnagogic states. Hypnagogic or hypnopompic hallucinations are visual, tactile, auditory, or other sensory events, usually brief but occasionally prolonged, that occur during transition from wakefulness to sleep (hypnagogic) or from sleep to wakefulness (hypnopompic).

These altered states of consciousness during transitional phases of going to sleep or waking up include lucid dreaming, hallucinations, out-of-body experiences, and sleep paralysis. Most everyone has had an episode of drifting off and starting to dream, only to suddenly jerk awake because your body wasn't totally paralyzed yet to keep you from acting out your dream and hurting yourself. We go into greater detail later, but suffice it to say that in an altered state, you would not suddenly acquire an unknown scar on your leg that was not there the day before. It would be a freshly scabbed wound, not a scar. People report appearances of healed scars. Some report that their nightgown or clothing was on backward and somehow was buttoned up the back, or they have tree leaves stuck between their toes from a 45-foot tree outside their bedroom window (and the lowest limbs are 10 feet off the ground), from an altered state. In other words, if you are sleepwalking, you will not have leaves between your toes from a tree you cannot reach, be dressed wrong with buttons you cannot reach even while awake, or have miraculously healed scars from bumping into sharp objects while asleep. Then again, that's just our opinion; we could be wrong. (A special thank you to Dennis Miller, the Master of the Rant.)

CONTACT WITH NONHUMAN LIFE FORMS

The abduction of human beings is something that arguably may have been going on for centuries. Stories of life forms coming out of the sky are in the Bible as Ezekiel's Wheel, and Native American tribes describe the sky people coming down to see them. If the cave drawings that suggest flying craft and creatures with helmets are to be believed, contact has been going on for a long, long time. After all, maybe we are just the late bloomers of the galaxy.

During the 1950s, a number of people came forward claiming alien contact and came to be known as contactees. Contactees claimed visitations and exchanges of information with beings from other planets, beginning with George Adamski in 1952. The stereotypical contactee account of the day involved not just communication but visits inside flying saucers and rides, often to a larger "Mother Ship" in orbit, and even trips to the moon, Venus, Mars, and Saturn.

04

THE ABDUCTIONS START

THE FIRST REPORTED CASE OF ALIEN ABDUCTION was that of Antonio Villas Boas in Brazil. Boas was a Brazilian farmer who claimed to have been abducted by extraterrestrials in 1957 while working on a farm. The twenty-three-year-old farmer was working at night to avoid the high daily temperatures. On October 16, 1957, he saw what he described as a "red star" in the sky. He watched as this star approached his position, increasing in size until it became recognizable as a roughly circular-shaped aerial craft, with red lights and a rotating cupola on top. The craft landed in the field on three extended legs. At that point, Boas attempted to leave the scene on his tractor, but when its lights and engine died after traveling only a very short distance, he began running on foot. However, he was grabbed by a 5-foot-tall humanoid who was wearing gray coveralls and what Boas determined was a space helmet. The entity's eyes were small and blue, and instead of some type of speech, it made a barking sound or yelps like an animal. Three similar beings then joined in dragging him inside their craft.

This was the first case where a person had been forcibly taken and machinery had been shut down to prevent escape from the scene of the abduction. These creatures were not your typically reported type, and the whole thing may have been random, sort of like: "Hey, there's one now; let's get *him*!" However, it gets stranger.

Once dragged inside the craft, he was stripped of his clothes and covered from head to toe with a strange gel, which one might think would be a disinfectant in an effort to not transmit an earthly disease to the craft's occupants. He was then led into a large semicircular room. In this room the entities took samples of blood from his chin. After this, he was taken to a third room and left alone for what seemed like half an hour (just like our typical doctor's office—take a sample, then hurry up and wait). During this time, some kind of gas was pumped into the room that made him violently ill. This might have been some type of attempt to sterilize his lungs, so that he wouldn't breathe out something like the common cold bug and infect them, or maybe it was to sedate him for whatever was coming next.

Boas was then joined in the room by another humanoid. This one was female . . . and naked. She was the same size and had a small, pointed chin but large, blue catlike eyes. Large eyes always seem to be the theme in latter-day abduction reports. Boas said the hair on her head was long and white, but her underarm and pubic hair were bright red. Boas commented that she was very attractive. And that he was strongly attracted to her. We never met Boas, but this behavior seems a little bit strange considering he saw a spaceship land, was grabbed against his will by aliens, was stripped naked, and now is feeling attracted to a naked female crew member of this craft . . . (Just trying to sum things up and put in some perspective here.) And then, the two had sexual intercourse. Not something we would see space aliens doing to us or we to them. Did this apparently seem like a good idea at the time to Boas, or was Boas's mind and actions being controlled by other forces? When it was all over, the female smiled at Boas, rubbing her belly and gesturing upward. Boas took this to mean that she was going to raise their child in space. He was angered because he felt as though he had been little more than "a good stallion." He was given back his clothing and, after a short tour of the craft, was then escorted off the ship and watched as it took off, brightly glowing. Boas returned home and discovered that four hours had passed. He died in 1992 and stuck to the story of his alleged abduction for the rest of his life.

From the beginning, not all aspects of this abduction were as they are now. The Boas case had different beings than are typical today, and they manually chased him down to catch him. Granted, it was 1957, and maybe these beings weren't really as advanced as the ones doing the abducting now. They did exhibit the ability to control his tractor, just as happens today. Sexual intercourse, while not something most people would think would be part of this scenario, does happen. Sometimes, sexual intercourse happens with modified alien beings or hybrids, and sometimes with other abductees. His memory of the event was always intact, unlike some of today's abductions, which often involve periods of no memory, missing time, or only bits and pieces of memory available about the event. Perhaps we are easier to catch the second time if we don't remember the first!

Mind Games and Guilt

We once worked with a fellow who was forced on a regular basis to have sex with another female abductee aboard a UFO. He had never met her anywhere other than aboard a craft and felt terrible about it. He was horrified that he was cheating on his wife with this other abductee. He felt that their unions had resulted in children, although he was never shown any, which made it even worse. We have been witnesses at a UFO conference where two abductees met for the first time in our everyday world—they'd known each other from aboard a craft and had been abducted together multiple times over a period of years. It was like watching two long-lost friends or, in some cases, long-lost lovers.

Do they share emotions of a traumatic situation? Or of a joint manipulation? Or both? All abductees share a unique bond. It's like an intimate hard-wiring, if you will. They feel each other's presence and connection. It is touching to see. While not trying to take anything away from the intimacy of these connections, one must ask if they are genuine feelings or ones that have been somehow programmed into the psyche of the abductee to make the process easier somehow.

Intimacy Onboard a Craft: Controlled Reproduction for Harvest

Please understand that abductees do not have much, if any, control in this situation. Sex is hard-wired into our systems anyway, and these beings seem very adept at circumventing personal feelings such as guilt. It is like the abductees' bodies are on autopilot, and they have intercourse. We have had it explained as absolutely not enjoyable and very mechanical in nature, almost like there is an unseen element at work in collecting semen and ova during their intercourse and that they were just going through the motions. In some cases, it seems like the act is in their head only, and other things unknown to them are going on externally. The main point here is they are being controlled.

Mainstream US Media Meets the Hill Abduction Case

What started the whole alien abduction interest in the US was the Hill abduction of 1961. Betty and Barney Hill were abducted by creatures on their way home one night from a vacation while driving through the White Mountains of New Hampshire, and their story and the investigation were brought to light in the 1966 book by John G. Fuller called *Interrupted Journey*. Excerpts of Fuller's book and the Hills' story made the cover of *LOOK* magazine, a very popular magazine of the day. We met Betty, as she was one of our guest speakers at the 2002 MUFON International Symposium in Rochester, New York, and she told us her story.

She was one feisty little wisp of a woman who had lived through a very strange experience with her husband, Barney. While she lost Barney in 1969, Betty continued to look for answers and toured the world as a guest speaker till her passing. She was not afraid of her experience and appeared extremely inquisitive about her abductors. When she toured, she told the world about what was out there. She was by far the most popular speaker at the symposium that year, with a good share of the 300-seat audience there to see just her. It was surely a treat to finally meet her. Betty sadly passed away at the age of eighty-five in 2004. Her memory and cause live on.

In 1964, New York City painter and sculptor Budd Hopkins had a daytime sighting of a UFO with two other witnesses, and it sparked an interest and curiosity within him. He joined National Investigations Committee on Aerial Phenomena (NICAP) (now defunct). He continued to learn about the topic until 1975, when he and Ted Bloecher, another well-known UFO investigator of the time, began studying a North Hudson Park UFO sighting with multiple witnesses.

In 1976, the *Village Voice*, a New York newspaper, printed an account of Budd Hopkins's investigation of the park sighting. It wasn't long before Budd was receiving letters from other witnesses of other UFO sightings, some with periods of missing time that they could not explain in any rational way. Budd's spark became a flame.

In 1981, Budd published *Missing Time*. The book was the first real study of the alien abduction phenomenon, covering multiple cases of abduction. Budd did not like the fact that people were being taken against their will by nonhuman entities. He went on to become the most notable alien abduction researcher in the world, writing the additional books *Intruders* (1987), *Witnessed* (1996), and *Sight Unseen* (2003), and he founded the Intruders Foundation (1989) in New York City. "IF," as it was called, was not just a research and investigation group run by Budd, but a place where one could find support and safety with other people who had suffered the same frightening experience. Having had the experience of participating in one of Budd's groups and a super-rare chance to be accepted inside the fold and observe Budd do hypnotic regressions on one of my longtime abductees was fascinating. Budd passed in August 2011. His cause marches on within all of us, and we will miss him. The year 1987 brought Budd's second book, *Intruders*, and another newcomer to the world of alien abduction: author Whitley Strieber.

Strieber lived in New York at the time and was an accomplished author of horror novels. He had a cabin in upstate New York, where he liked to spend time with family and friends, but he became aware of odd happenings when he stayed there. Due to a very strange December 26, 1985, night, his saga began with strange dreams, bright lights in the sky over his house, and disturbing flashes of memories. He had feelings that someone had broken into the house, followed by nothing short of paranoia.

Whitley thought that perhaps he was starting to lose his mind or maybe had a brain tumor or something of that nature. He went for help. Going through a battery of medical tests, he was cleared of anything physically wrong with him; his search continued. A psychiatrist he went to see suggested hypnotic regression to see what might be the cause of all of Whitley's anxiety. What came out of Whitley Strieber's memories filled the pages and the cover of his then-new nonfiction book *Communion*.

The cover showed an artist's rendering of the beings that Whitley had memories of, the now-infamous Grey aliens with the big, black, almond-shaped eyes. The book was a ticking time bomb for some. While most glanced at it and put it down, some people were strangely transfixed by the cover. Those large, black, glistening, almond-shaped eyes brought chills to some and heart palpitations to others. The book brought uncomfortable flashbacks and anxiety to some of those who bought it. In our opinion, this book was the largest single event to bring the topic of alien abduction to light. It was a trigger. It brought about sudden, shocking, fragmented memories of strange dreams featuring creatures with these big black eyes. The number of people who found the cover of this book disturbing was *huge*. Something was going on. People would be walking along the sidewalk and glance in the bookstore window to see *Communion* on display, see those black, bottomless eyes looking back at them, and experience a shot of adrenaline. Not understanding the magnitude of the jolt, they bought the book in droves. Many read the book; some could not. We have been in the homes of abductees and seen Whitley's *Communion* on the shelf; mostly unread, with a scrap of paper as a bookmark a few pages in. That's where the reader got uncomfortable for some unknown reason and put the book down.

I personally (Bob) remember one woman—we will call her "Ella"—who owned approximately twenty books on UFOs and alien abduction. Every book had a bookmark within the first fifty pages or so. Some of them she had owned for years. She had not, to my knowledge, ever read a book on that topic to the end. She would get freaked out and put it down—although this did not fully stop her from buying the next one she eyed at the bookstore. Something always drew her back to buying more of them. Now a longtime friend of mine, and abductee, she has never stopped looking for answers.

It Runs in the Family

While not initially realized, it was considered later that abductions followed along family lines, suggesting that DNA markers had something to do with the chances of being abducted. Abductions involving families with histories of UFO sightings became commonplace, in fact. People reporting not abductions but UFO sightings would mention that their mom or dad had seen them years before, or even that Grandpa had a UFO hover over him while out in the field, planting corn. When this first came to light, it sent a shockwave through all abductees who were parents. We've heard gripping stories told by parents of missing children, only to find them back in their beds with stories of the little doctors that came to see them.

For years now, since the 1950s, abduction reports filtered in where semen and ovum samples were being taken, often with traumatic results to the abductee. Initially these facts were even left out of abduction reports; such details were thought just too disturbing or embarrassing for the victim. Barney Hill, Betty's husband, was traumatized by just such an event, one he did not want to disclose even to investigators much less anyone else, understandably.

These abductions became personally invasive. Women would be placed on a table, and a very long needle would be placed into them to extract ova. Sometimes mock sexual interludes were contrived to express semen from men. Some abductees were forced to have sexual relations with other abductees while aboard the craft, usually with a group of Greys observing and collecting samples. Since these beings are stealing our genetic material without our consent, it stands to reason that they continue to follow the genetic lines they need or prefer, opening too much speculation as to why they are collecting it.

We see the children of abductees having abductions. If the people who answered the Roper poll with a positive group of answers back in 1991—strongly suggesting that they had been abducted, and they had children at that time, then now, over twenty years later, those children have grown up and are having children of their own, and the abduction phenomenon continues with the new children—how many more people are being abducted from the original 1991 figure of well over 3.5 million American citizens?

We are being controlled. We are being bred. Our very personal property is being taken. We are being cut open, probed, implanted, and used as growing chambers, and then having fetuses harvested from our wombs. Sound crazy? It's old news, really. It's been going on for over fifty years at this point. What? You missed all of this? It's been there all the time for anyone who really wanted to look. What is new is that we are getting smarter. We want our control back. Organizations such as MUFON (Mutual UFO Network) are getting better people. Better organized and funded. Abductees have formed groups to share ideas and heal one another. Our technology is presenting quantum clues to how they may control us or how the curtain of the impossible may be lifted. Our species will always break its bonds and surprise. I can't wait to see it in their eyes!

ANECDOTAL EVIDENCE

We would like to touch for just a second on something that the late Dr. John E. Mack, professor of psychiatry at the Cambridge Hospital, Harvard Medical School, and founding director of the Center for Psychology and Social Change, had to say about anecdotal evidence.

Having met Dr. John Mack a couple of times in the very early '90s and having had a chance to participate in a couple of his conferences, he would talk about how the skeptics often downplayed the significance of what they called "anecdotal evidence." He stated, "Anecdotal evidence translates as human experience." He said that in today's legal system, witness testimony is presented to a jury for deliberation. The often-anecdotal evidence of an eyewitness can send a proposed felon to be sentenced to death if the charge is severe enough.

The late Budd Hopkins developed this line of thought further with the analogy of how expert witnesses are required to present laboratory findings to a jury in criminal cases, and that the physical evidence, such as DNA or chemical evidence in these cases, is often never actually seen by the jury. The jury members depend on the testimony of others to present the information to them. Many "experts" now make a living giving high-priced testimony in court cases. The point being made here is that almost all physical evidence is, in some sense of the word, anecdotal and depends on our ability to trust who is telling us about it. Since, over the years, many reported abductees have passed polygraph tests with flying colors, this suggests that they are not being deceptive and that they believe the information they are relaying to the researcher.

Beyond the hype and commercialism lies the real source of input of what we know so far: anecdotal evidence by the people directly involved with the phenomena. They are strange beings that force our paradigm to change how we see the world or worlds and how we function in our everyday lives. Our normal world is turned upside down, giving way to the most bizarre life-changing circumstances. They commonly come like thieves in the night to stun and confound. Like demons under the cover of darkness, they take their intended victim. In fact, how do we not know that they are the source of demon stories throughout history?

Side note here: Years ago, I (Bob) suggested to a Christian counselor friend of mine to read a copy of Mack's *Abduction* for her take on it. Upon reading the book, I asked her what she thought, and her reply was "They seem more like demons to me."

Demons or not, they maintain control. They make their existence to the known world questionable. They don't land on the White House lawn, they don't appear in the noonday sky before everyone, and they don't say that they "come in peace." They are deceptive and sneaky and treat us like cattle. They take from us our own cells and use them to raise hybrid babies that are a cross of human and whatever they are. They abduct mothers and implant altered fetuses and then remove the fetuses in a later abductions. Women are abducted and forced into holding these limp, lifeless, and mostly hairless hybrids. And worst of all, they abduct our own natural children and start the indoctrination process all over again. They just wait for your child to become productive and fertile, to once again begin the alien harvest.

If we sound dramatic, it is because we have worked with and studied a large collective group of people over the years that are experiencing being abducted. They write us, call us, and come to us with fear and bewilderment. They fear the night, the solitude of feeling like the only one. They have the fear of being thought disturbed or crazy. To some, a preferable thought. We have seen the fear in their eyes. We have conversed with a few about aliens taking their children. We have seen people looking into why they have what seem like irrational fears, suddenly bursting into tears and screaming with terror because a memory of something much unexpected broke loose during questioning.

Bob:

I once had a casual conversation with a fellow who was interested in UFOs while visiting his place of employment. It had come up in conversation while I was waiting there, and he wanted to talk more about UFOs. I explained that my primary interest was the phenomenon of abduction. He seemed quite interested, so we planned to meet for lunch and discuss it further.

We met, not far from his job, and sat down to enjoy a sub from the corner deli. We will call him Andy. Andy did not claim to be an abductee or show any special interest in that end of the topic and in fact had to his knowledge never seen an unidentified flying object but had always wanted to see one.

I explained that I had studied the abduction phenomenon for twenty years, and showed him a drawing of a Grey alien done by an abductee. The first words out of his mouth were "That's not what the eyes look like; the eyes are wrong." I looked at him, and he had this really troubled and visibly shaken look. I ask what was wrong, and he just stared at the picture. I again ask him if he was okay, and he turns to me, now slightly pale and really rattled, and said, "The eyes are wrong . . . how would I know that?"

In my head, I'm thinking red flags; on the outside I remained cool. Either this guy is trying to pull one over on me and give me some rope to run with, or something out of left field knocked him for a loop. I played it cool and suggested that in today's culture, images of artistic portrayals of alien heads are everywhere, including commercials. I would be hard to go through the typical day without seeing such an image from bumper stickers to candy containers; of course they always make them green instead of Grey, but you get my point.

He thought for a minute and then insisted that he had never seen one or been abducted, and the whole notion was just ridiculous. I said that was fine, and just forget the whole thing. People draw the eyes several ways with different slants, and since memory is so often affected, lots of discrepancies exist. They were probably different from the last alien movie he had seen or something and thought nothing more of it externally.

He left shortly after that. I found out that in the following week, his email address no longer existed, his phone was disconnected, and since

I had met him at his place of work, I stopped in only to find out he had quit his job that same day. Just gone! Even freaked me out just a little, and I deal with strange every day.

I would hazard a guess that maybe he had seen something, and it was floating around in his subconscious mind. The picture he was looking at brought it forward, and down the rabbit hole he went. It works like that sometimes.

Researchers must always remain objective. They must be logical and ethical and have a healthy dose of skepticism, but after reliving some of these experiences through the people we have worked with, it is sometimes hard not to feel for them on an emotional level.

Professional counselors have private retreats where they get to talk with other counselors to unload the baggage that accumulates from constant counseling emotions piling up. We do our best to remain objective at all times and be scientific and follow protocol set forth by investigative organizations such as the Mutual UFO Network Inc.(MUFON). MUFON members are required to study and pass qualification tests to become a MUFON investigator.

We feel for abductees. They're not just a case number or something to be slid under a microscope, while being poked and prodded. They're one of us. They're human—a condition we hold precious, especially now.

THE CREATURES WHO ABDUCT HUMANS

Primary Offenders: The Short Greys

Descriptions of the short Greys are taken from personal testimony of abductees we have worked with, the proceedings of the Abduction Study Conference held at MIT, and *UFO Abductions: The Measure of a Mystery* by Thomas E. Bullard for the Fund for UFO Research, plus several other books on the subject.

These small creatures are the workers of the abduction phenomenon: the escort service, if you will. They range in size from 3 to 4 feet tall. Frail-appearing bodies with large bulbous heads rest on necks that seems like they would snap like a twig because of the disproportionate size to the head. The neck does not seem to house any swallowing tube, and no Adam's apple is present. The shape of the head has been compared to a pear, egg, or teardrop shape, with a pointed chin but no visible jawbone. The cover of the book *Communion* showed Whitley Strieber's memory of what his captors looked like: a typical Grey but with a smaller cranium. The eyes were the same, and I think it was the eyes that caused most of the recognition factor.

As mentioned, most are reported to have very large bulbous heads, and the eyes of course are what set everybody off with the *Communion* cover.

The large compelling eyes of the Greys capture attention like no other bodily feature. The size and hypnotic attraction of these organs prefigure their role as instruments of control over the witness. Large, pitch-black, almond-shaped eyes. No discernible eyelashes, eyebrows, or eyelids. No pupils or iris, just black, glistening, motionless eyes. There have been a few reports that some abductees have seen a pupil, and that it was covered by a black contact-type lens cover. This type of report is rare and may or may not be the case.

The cranial surface is gray and bald with no visible hair, just like the rest of the creature's body. The other expected orifices of the head appear vestigial. No visible ears, but perhaps just a hole. The nose consists of a slight ridge and two holes with no protrusion from the head. And the mouth just seems to be a lipless slit that is used neither for vocal communications nor eating. The mouths don't move, and no musculature of the head and face seems evident. There are no facial expressions usually reported. Faces are immobile, expressionless, and inscrutable, such that they reveal nothing to the witness. Bodies appear small and out of proportion to the head. The body is not bifurcated, and no bone understructure is evident. No spine, no ribs, and no musculature bulges. Abductees report not feeling any air exhaled from the facial area during very close procedures, and the chest does not rise and fall as if there are expanding and contracting lungs. The clear majority of the small Greys appear the same height and weight, almost as if stamped out by a cookie cutter. It has been suggested that they are clones and have a hive mentality like worker bees. Abductees report that they get a feeling that some Greys are male, while others female, although there is no outward bodywise difference between perceived sexes. There are no breasts, nipples, or external genitalia present. Similarly, there appears to be no buttocks or rectum on a small Grey. Arm diameter is the same from the shoulder to the hand, the legs hang down directly from the torso, and thighs are the same diameter as where the feet join. Little is known about the feet; some people report a protective covering on them, while most never get the chance to observe the feet. The hands are reported to be large for the arm diameter, with three or four long, spindly fingers. The skin is most often gray in color with no pores, wrinkles, or hair. The skin is also described as rubbery, with no apparent veins, bumps, warts, blemishes, or skin imperfections like humans.

One abductee I (Bob) personally worked with said that their skin reminded him of a fungus, like the surface of a mushroom, and felt cold and rubbery to that effect. Throughout most abductions the beings maintain an unconcerned and clinical aloofness, an image of unfeeling and cerebral impassiveness, unperturbed even when angry witnesses strike blows to them. They are also ever evasive. When a witness questions the beings, the witness gets the silent treatment as they simply ignore any inquiry. Any response is vague, evasive, and at best a partial answer to half-satisfy the abductee to comply with whatever procedure is being done, but in fact divulges nothing. They do not seem to like being stared at or studied either, and such behavior is not allowed.

05

STATISTICAL RESEARCH AND ALIEN ABDUCTIONS

DR. THOMAS E. BULLARD, A FOLKLORIST AND UFO researcher, conducted a study of hundreds of UFO abduction cases, looking as far back as the 1950s. In his research he found several patterns emerging. These patterns became a chronology of events that occur in a majority of alien abduction scenarios. Numerous alien abduction researchers contributed cases to Dr. Bullard's study. We would like to acknowledge the tremendous volume of cases and time that he put into his study, and thank him for allowing us to present some of his findings in this book.

THE WHEAT FROM THE CHAFF

With literally thousands of reported abduction cases from all around the world, not all abductions fit into the same mold. Abductions that have a certain set of qualifications are usually investigated, while many lesser ones are not. It depends on when and where they come to light, and the manpower available to offer a reliable investigation and scientific analysis of the data gleaned from it.

About 95 percent of all reported UFO sightings are attributable to natural aerial phenomena that are misidentified, or misidentification of known or classified aircraft. The last 5 percent of reported sightings fall into the category of being a true unknown, often not only with witnesses but possibly including such data as radar history or a video capture. Digital cameras on phones are everywhere, and more stuff is being captured during witnessed events. Another control issue is the fact that electronics have a high failure rate in close proximity to a UFO. I would imagine that this is by design to keep the UFO encounter as secretive as possible. We go into this in greater detail later in the book.

Reported abduction cases are different from sighting reports. We would say that the percentage of cases with a high probability of some type of nonhuman contact is much higher than the 5 percent of true unknown sighting reports. Someone reporting an abduction case can potentially set themselves up for negative publicity, ridicule, and just more trouble with the risk of discovery than they sometimes bargained for. We would like to thank the brave individuals who do come forth and share their stories with sometimes crucial information.

The Chaff

Obviously, some abduction reports are hoaxes by people, and while we have a sense of humor, we find that they apparently have too much time on their hands and tend to waste our valuable and very limited resources. Some abduction reports are related to psychological pathology or misunderstood biological anomalies such as sleep paralysis, which the debunkers so like to pigeonhole the entire abduction phenomenon into. It's sort of like the "If you have ever been drunk, then you must be Irish" type of logic. These people say, "If you have ever had an abduction experience, then you suffer from sleep paralysis or 'Old Hag Syndrome.'"

"Old Hag Syndrome"

The name of this phenomenon comes from the superstition that an "Old Hag "or "Witch" is sitting on the chest of her victim, rendering them paralyzed and making it hard for them to breathe. This is obviously not taken very seriously in that respect in today's world, but it was taken seriously 250 years ago. Today, the phenomenon still exists, and while it is much better understood, it is still quite frightening in nature to someone experiencing it, and, again, cultural beliefs may play a factor into the level of reality one may experience regarding the subjects of ghosts, witches, demons, and the supernatural.

The experience of sleep paralysis is frightening because the person is awake but paralyzed. The individual *seems* to have complete use of their senses, including being able to see shadowy apparitions, experience strange smells, sense feelings of doom or evil, or feel a sensation of pressure on their chest, as if something is on them. The person's senses are telling them that something real and unusual is happening to them.

What is happening is that when the brain is in the transition state between deep, dreaming sleep, known as rapid eye movement (REM) sleep, and waking up, the brain has turned off most of the body's muscle function, so we cannot act out our dreams and hurt ourselves, making us temporarily paralyzed. The switching process is largely a group of chemical reactions in the brain that can sometimes take longer than normal to realize, resulting in a groggy, hypnopompic state with muscle paralysis. Once the person has come out of the altered state of consciousness, fully awake and well, they are completely baffled by what just happened to them. It's not surprising that this stuff gets mixed and mingled with abduction experiences. With such a bizarre and irrational experience, it's no wonder that many victims fear that they have been attacked in their bed. However, there are some basic differences between the two that make for an easy distinction.

The difference is that they never experience being abducted in sleep paralysis. Sleep paralysis does not have you removed from your house (or car for that matter) and taken into some imaginary craft from a hypnopompic state. In sleep paralysis, you stay in your bed. Sleep paralysis experiencers do not wake with physical scars or anomalous metallic objects that show up on X-rays. And the neighbors never report seeing a UFO in your backyard during sleep paralysis. Bottom line: Sleep paralysis is very real, but not to be confused with an abduction experience.

"Dreams"

Steven Pinker is a Canadian American cognitive scientist, psychologist, linguist, and popular-science author. He stated that "the mind is a product of the brain, that the brain is organized in part by the genome, and that the genome was shaped by natural selection." He makes this distinction between the brain and the mind that the brain is an organ; the mind is what that organ does. Here we are dealing with the full power of the mind and its creativity.

Everyone has had a strange or bizarre dream. More than you can count or remember, in fact. It can make your heart pound and sometimes even force you to awaken in a burst of panic. Why? Because your dream is real to you, until it isn't. The filters are off and anything is possible—until you wake and then the conscious mind comes back online and lets you discern that it wasn't real; it was just a dream.

Misinterpretations of Dreams

Dreams usually happen when a person is in REM sleep. Most dreams are a construct from a mixture of recent daily events and people. As stated above, anything is possible for the subconscious mind during a dream state. In the case of an alien abduction event, a dream may be a sort of message sent from the subconscious mind to the conscious—to bring it forward to a state where it can be processed.

I (Jim) met with a woman who tells of a dream in which she was taken by a Grey being and led through a wooded area to a landed UFO. The woman said that in the dream she was wearing only a nightgown and no shoes, and when she walked in the woods she could feel the stones and twigs on the ground, and they hurt her feet. When they approached the UFO, there was a reptilian-looking being there who began to yell and reprimand the Grey being, saying that he should not have brought her there. They could not use her, since she could not biologically bear children. The woman, although not pleased with being taken, did feel some sympathy for the Grey being for getting yelled at by the other being.

Was this a dream? Or was it an abduction event disguised as a dream memory? We believe that in some circumstances, some very odd yet vivid dreams recall abduction events that have happened in the past and that have been hidden from conscious memory.

Can someone watch a science fiction movie that contains an alien abduction scene and have a dream about it? Sure! Except that dream is totally based on fiction and will have distortions because of being constructed within the subconscious mind.

Have you ever had a dream of flying? Yeah, us too! It is one of the most common dreams, along with going to school and forgetting your pants, and that is all it is. It does not mean that they all have had abduction experiences. People who have experienced an abduction event, however, do frequently have memories of being floated up a beam of light to a waiting ship, which certainly seems like flying and results as a dreamlike flying sequence.

It is certainly possible to have a dream about being abducted by aliens. In fact, many people who are seasoned abductees still refer to what they remember as a dream. The term "dream" has a safety factor to it. Dreams aren't real.

There are very easy ways to differentiate between dreams and events of a more real nature. In a dream, you may be in your bedroom; it is not the same size as your bedroom, and the walls are a different color. There is a different bed, a fountain pool with purple koi fish, and a talking orangutan that speaks fluent German. Okay, so you might ask yourself what you had as a bedtime snack. But our point is that dreams go outside the box, and yet everything seems completely natural. It feels like your bedroom even though it is nothing like your room, because the subconscious takes everything at face value and does not judge or evaluate. It just is. This is a dream. When you wake, the conscious mind kicks in and says, "Wow, what a weird dream!" The point is that it is easy to tell what you just experienced is not how things really are.

During a fragmented memory of an abduction, your room is still your room, just as it really is. Same bed, same colors, same furniture. Nothing is different except for possibly a group of maybe three short Grey aliens with big heads and large, black, almond-shaped eyes looking at you. No orangutans or koi fish, and you are not being chased by them because that is not the reality of the experience. There is a high probability, in our opinion, that it is not a dream but a fragment of a memory.

That is not to say that a real physical experience (of any type) cannot instantly affect a dream you might have. Have you ever dreamt that you were falling, and suddenly your body hit the floor from rolling out of bed? In the split second between rolling out of bed and traveling the very short distance to the floor, your brain concocted a dream about falling from the feeling of the sensory input. Time means nothing in an altered state of reality. Travis Walton, from Snowflake, Arizona, was abducted November 5, 1975, and was gone for five days. Upon return, he thought he had been gone just a matter of hours. That 3-pound universe between your ears is pretty cool equipment, but apparently it can be controlled to a certain extent and manipulated.

As an investigator, you will find out that sometimes you have to separate the wheat from the chaff. Lots of things can alter perceptions of an experience or event, such as drugs, alcohol, disease, allergies, belief systems, etc. Never assume an abduction event has occurred. Rule out every other possibility, including a hoax. Be as scientific and objective as possible. Like the saying goes, "I want to believe." Don't let yourself go down that road. Healthy skepticism is a useful tool.

CULTURAL BELIEFS

Some cultural belief systems play a part in the objectivity of a report; for example, Native American elders from almost every tribe from Pawnee to the Iroquois have stories of star people or sky spirits. In Native American storytelling traditions dating back to antiquity, the gods would come down from heaven to impregnate females in small, remote villages. Women bearing these strange "Star Children" would raise them as their own until the age of five or six, when the sky gods would return to claim them, leaving the parents who had raised them staring up at the night sky and wondering. This could have certainly happened if you compare it to today's same circumstances and scenarios involving abduction. At that time, Native Americans may have accepted the abduction of their "star child" just a little easier than, say, today's parents, if for no other reason than it being the will of the gods. It may even have been considered by some, an honor to have raised a "Star Child."

These cultural stories span almost every tribe, coast to coast. Are these just stories handed down from generation to generation, powered by their belief system? *Or*, was there some type of alien infiltration and control already happening way before stories of contact and abduction came to light in the 1950s and '60s?

06

THE TYPICAL ABDUCTION SCENARIO

ONCE RESEARCHERS STARTED TO ACCUMULATE A LARGER number of abduction cases, it became obvious that there were patterns in many that matched up perfectly with other cases, from people who did not know each other and from different parts of the country and the world. This was long before the internet and the fast dissemination of information (or disinformation), and before all the published abduction books and made-for-TV movies about it. A majority of the cases that we looked at have a marked series of similar patterns that become familiar to the researchers and investigators. We will attempt to sum up the major events chronologically and run through these to give the reader who is unfamiliar with it a basic understanding. We will also address the largest factor with getting reliable intelligence about the experience of abduction.

Doorway Amnesia

An alien abduction usually starts out with an unsuspecting individual who knows nothing of what *will* happen and ends up as a confused victim who knows little or nothing of what *did* happen to them, due to a manipulation of their memory of the event. The event may start with the sighting of a strange light in the sky or even a daylight sighting of a craft, often in close proximity to the person (i.e., a close encounter). Their next memory may be of seeing this light in the sky or craft flying away, just as if it was there for a few seconds and then flew off.

Initially, someone who experienced an alien abduction may feel like something has happened to them, but it may be just a vague notion. It is commonly referred to as doorway amnesia. While being taken, having procedures done to them aboard a craft and up till the final goodbyes, so to speak, the abductee can remember most if not all of it. As soon as the abductee is removed from the alien craft, their memory of the event seems to be erased or certainly buried deep within their subconscious. This may be done either for the protection of the abductee, which initially might seem humane (i.e., protecting them from a traumatic memory), *or* to help keep the whole procedure as stealthy as possible (clandestine). We guess it depends on your point of view. I've known researchers who have been accused of being negative or painting it as a bad experience. We tend to look at it this way: If it looks like a duck, quacks like a duck, has feathers like a duck, but tells you it is a wildebeest, then what is it? Answer: a lying duck!

Traumatic memories never seem to remain hidden forever. At some point, a realization event occurs and a vivid flash of memory happens that causes the person to question what they had just experienced. The realization events creep back out of the subconscious where everything is stored and pop up into our everyday lives. The events are what prompt some to seek information and help regarding these stray, errant memories. They start to examine why they might be having them. Sometimes an abduction scenario crops up.

Author Whitley Strieber's account of his abduction experiences started out with him going to his doctor, thinking he had a mental disorder rearing its head or a brain tumor or something else that was causing what he was experiencing.

For some, the prospect of not knowing or understanding these flashbacks or triggers is the major cause of the anxiety. For others, seeking help in understanding and retrieving memories and finding you are or have been taken by nonhuman entities for some type of experiment in and of itself is traumatic. The act of now knowing it is a great relief to some. One of the subjects mentioned in this book, Frank, is one of those people. He was hypnotically regressed by Budd Hopkins, and it was as if a great weight had been lifted off him when his abduction experience came to light. He could then fortify himself and do away with the daily anxiety and frustration of not knowing what happened, which plagued him incessantly.

For those who think that regressive hypnosis is the only way to remember what has happened to them, that is not always the case. Many people have had conscious memories without having to retrieve them; in fact, many people have had flashbacks just like a Vietnam or Middle East vet might experience with PTSD. Posttraumatic stress disorder is a severe anxiety disorder that can develop after exposure to any event that results in psychological trauma. This event may involve the threat of death to oneself or to someone else, or to one's own or someone else's physical, sexual, or psychological integrity, overwhelming the individual's ability to cope

(*Diagnostic and Statistical Manual of Mental Disorders: DSM-IV*, Washington, DC: American Psychiatric Association, 1994). Certain triggers rattle loose a similar happening aboard an alien craft, and bits and pieces come flowing back. It may feel as if the abductee has had an awful dream that was somehow more than just that. Confusion between reality and nonreality gets blurred. Missing segments of time seem to occur, and it seems as if instead of sleeping, something else had happened, with no idea of what that was. The person may feel anxious, queasy, or sick.

When a person is abducted, no permission is given and they are taken against their will. The difference between a kidnapping and abduction is that an abduction victim is returned, usually in about two to three hours, generally unharmed physically, although they may be returned with a scar or biopsy mark of unknown origin, and there is never a ransom or a demand made to return them. Mentally, it can be a haunting experience.

There are three general phases to an alien abduction. It begins with the subject being taken (the capture). The victim may be sleeping at home, watching television, driving somewhere, or doing almost any normal daily activity. The person might start to notice a change in the area surrounding them. The subject may initially notice absences of all surrounding ambient sound or a temperature change; for example, one might be abducted and taken outside their dwelling to a waiting craft during the winter and feel no temperature change on their skin, even though they are only in their pajamas, at best, which is sometimes referred to as the Oz effect, a term coined by British researcher Jenny Randle back in the '80s. The area may become very static and quiet. Traffic from a local highway may be silent, even with cars passing by. In some cases, people nearby seem frozen in place, like statues.

We have always wondered about this phenomenon. Are the people really frozen in place or is the perception of the person being targeted changing due to the abduction process? Is it a time/dimension issue or what is called "time dilation," a slowing down of time as per the laws of special relativity?

What we mean by that is this: These creatures may be from somewhere else, but not in the sense that we normally think of. We think distant planets in other solar systems, far away from here. We will get into this later, but basically, what if they are from another dimension or alternate universe, which has become increasingly possible in scientific theory. Maybe they were here all along, just out of phase with us, and the abduction process that makes a person see people frozen around them is part of the process of that person being pulled out of phase with our world so that the beings can interact with them.

Before the initial entrance of the beings and the capture, a feeling of anxiety often sets in for seemingly no logical reason. A humming or droning that can be heard and felt is reported and sometimes is said to feel almost like it is coming from within them. Without warning, the victim may be surrounded by a beam of blue-white light coming from somewhere. Paralysis is next to subdue the victim. A few victims who were outside reported a sudden bank of fog low to the ground, as if to provide cover for the impending Greys to come calling, such as with the Tujunga Canyon case (1953) in California, which Ann Druffel investigated (the Tujunga Canyon abductions).

The subject seemed to lose control of their will and did not try to resist what was happening. Paralysis of the body set in. The subject may have panicked but could only manage basic movement of the eyes and became aware of a presence entering the room or beings walking toward their vehicle. The experience may have seemed surreal and dreamlike. Shadowy figures sometimes moved with what seemed like incredible speed, either that or, because of an altered perception, it seemed that way.

The abductee may suddenly become calm and act as if in an altered state of consciousness and control. They may even get a sense of familiarity of the event or déjà vu. The person is then removed from their surroundings by these entities by floating them out of the house via a doorway, but this is not the most commonly reported method of removal from a home. The most common is often a very strange and unusual way that perplexes the person beyond words. They find themselves being moved through a solid object to the outside of the house—floated and transported through a solid wall, ceiling, or closed window to the outside. Once outside they are lifted by a beam of bluish-white light accompanied by the entities. They have the sensation of flying and can give details of the roof of their home and surroundings that they normally would not have a perspective of. But eventually they find themselves in a stranger place.

Inside the Craft

Another instance of doorway amnesia sometimes happens here. We have worked with people who remember the craft, the aliens, the beam, the floating to the craft, and a doorway opening up. From there, they go blank. We suspect it is an overload of their own system, blocking them from the trauma of the event or maybe an enhanced manipulation from the beings. They get to this point, and we have seen people come out from under regression automatically rather than confront a memory of what happens beyond that doorway.

They usually find themselves in a seemingly familiar place, a circular room like that of a hospital examining room but with none of the normal paraphernalia of a hospital. Déjà vu sets in again, and they are prepared for an examination. Their clothes are removed, and they are prepared to be studied. If they try to resist, they are put under submission by the aliens, usually by a touch to the head by the being's hand or by a small handheld device such as a wand or probe. (We hate using that word "probe," just because of all the baggage that comes with it regarding some abduction stories.) The person may have a staring procedure done with a taller lead alien. The lead alien is around 5 feet tall and seems to be the one in charge of the examination, as well as giving orders to the other smaller ones— although this is more perceived than actually heard.

Sometimes a pod or bar-type device is placed over the victim to scan the body, perhaps like an MRI or CAT scan that humans use. Various instrument types are used to probe the body. In very rare reports, a long, snakelike device comes out of the wall and is inserted into the rectum of the victim. Whitley Strieber's *Communion* TV movie included this, although we suspect it may have contaminated other reports due to the traumatic nature—like an anal rape. The process may have been to take samples of what we have eaten, or maybe to implant something within the victim. Like we said, it's rare, and we know little about its nature, although it certainly got into the alien abduction rumor mill and camp alien humor.

They take samples of the victim, maybe a part of the flesh, which leads to a scoop-like indentation on the person's skin, or samples of blood or other bodily fluids. They may feel and count the vertebrae in the spine. This has been reported numerous times. We don't know if they (the beings) even have a bone structure, as they seem to have a physique more like the clay animation figure "Gumby" than anything else. This may be followed by an examination of the reproductive organs by conducting tests and removing samples, or even closely monitored sexual interactions with another abductee of the opposite sex.

At some point, they may insert certain implants, which will be discussed in a later part of this book. It is believed by some that the implants play a large part in the control factor of the abductee as well as tracking—no different than us putting a tracking collar on a grizzly bear to monitor behavior. Bio-anomalies have shown up on PET and CAT scans—seemingly metal pellets or BBs implanted into the base of the brain, for example. These are impossible to remove without dire consequences to the person implanted, so we cannot truly study an implanted object. These just show up like a metal blip on the scan; other than that, we know nothing about them. We might also mention here that there are special helmets being made to block the transmissions from cranial implants, which we will touch on later. I know right now you are picturing a tin foil helmet and wondering why you bought this book. Turns out there may be something to it after all, and some abductees have had very positive responses from the helmets, especially while sleeping.

I (Bob) recall seeing a head X-ray that showed a metallic object in the sinuses of a woman. There have been reports of people sneezing and having something metallic fly out of their noses and roll across the floor. These objects have been saved in glass jars, only to evaporate into thin air shortly thereafter. How does one verify this? I don't know, but the stories keep coming. We put much more weight into the older reported events than the new ones, just because there is so much information on the internet. It makes it easy for someone to manufacture an experience and come forth with it, although there are still closely held clues to spotting a fake. Still, so much of our information is anecdotal in nature.

A final exam may be of the behavioral patterns of the victim. The person may be shown pictures of world devastation so as to illicit an emotional response. They are sometimes told that they are part of a bigger plan to save the world or the human race, or several different stories. The abductees' questions are never answered, and there is a subversive feeling to the whole thing.

There are several other things that may happen during the abduction. Not the same to all, but some may be taken on a trip to seemingly another planet. Or they are shown things that may happen in our future. They may be shown what appears to be an alien-human hybrid fetus or a small hybrid child. They may be taught things that they are to forget for now but that will be used in the future. Some are taught to pilot smaller craft and even participate in abductions of other people.

When all is done, they get the abductee ready for the return trip home or back to where they started. Unfortunately, they sometimes make mistakes and return people to different places or in different clothes. Budd Hopkins once worked with two people who were abducted together from different homes and, when brought back, were briefly put back into the wrong bedrooms. Even though their technology is impressive, they can make mistakes. The beings give the abductee a final message and bid them farewell. At this point the door of the craft is opened and the person is returned. As they move through the doorway, they undergo doorway amnesia and most everything is forgotten—for now. They forget all that happened, and when they get back to their bed or their car (wherever), they may think that only a few seconds or minutes have gone by, and they don't realize what has happened. However, if you experience too many instances of two or three hours of lost time, you start to question what's going on. Missing time events are often the founding cause leading to a realization event.

Sometimes, though, the abductee can recall the events and knows exactly what has happened. When returned, the abductee may see the craft leaving and think that they merely saw an unusual light in the sky for a moment, and then it left . . . leaving no understanding of what had occurred. The abductee then goes about his or her normal activity. Some might consider this as the perfect abduction—the one we don't remember. It doesn't change the fact that it is against our will, totally without permission.

Note on permission:

Some abductees are told that while they may not remember doing so, they did indeed give permission to the aliens to be abducted—perhaps long ago—and that this has been happening for years. That it is a necessary participation on the part of the abductee and they no longer have any say in the matter. Whether this is factual, an altered-state suggestion for abductees to believe, or just a plain lie we of course don't know.

Who Are the People Being Abducted?

Anybody with the right genetic traits the Greys are looking for. Any race, from any country on Earth, both sexes, and almost any age, with early childhood seen as a time of initiation to contact, and then with sexual maturity being prime age for abductions and the harvesting of reproductive cells.

The person being abducted could be you, your neighbor, your barber, your boss, or your loved one. It could be your own son or daughter. Sometimes the abduction phenomenon comes at you out of left field, and you never see it coming. It could be the cover of a book that creeps you out, and you don't know why. A flashback with surreal creatures that seems like a dream, but you wake up in the morning with a strange new scar. Or you have had multiple close sightings of a UFO.

If a husband and wife have had experiences of being abducted by aliens, then the chances are pretty good that their children will experience it also. They seem to follow along family lines as if they are studying family genetic makeup, or it's the family's genes that allow them to control you in the first place. Earlier we talked about Steven Pinker, and that the human genome is responsible for the brain's structure and function. Genetics play a role here somehow. Maybe some can't be controlled because of their genome, and others can because theirs is developed differently.

One instance comes from a couple we mention in this book a few times. I (Jim) have worked Frank and his wife, Miriam, many times over the years. Frank had videotaped a UFO flying over his town, and when he put the camcorder away, he forgot all about it and what had happened to him the rest of the night. He and his wife, who also saw the UFO, didn't discuss the event for eight days. This is a very common trait of the phenomenon. Multiple witnesses often have no desire to talk about their shared sighting and sometime treat it like it never happened, as if the suggestion to do so had been implanted into their subconscious mind by these creatures.

When he finally told her about the UFO, he was surprised to find out that she already knew about it and that she was there as well. When hypnotically regressed years later, he recalled being taken from his kitchen and going through the ceiling (removal through a solid object) and approaching the same UFO hovering over his house. Learning that he had been abducted did not surprise him or his wife, since they have had many UFO sightings and other encounters. They just never remember them consciously until one seems to either reach a saturation point in the experience or a trigger is hit that prompts a memory and an emotional response.

Earlier we mentioned Betty and Barney Hill. They were the New Hampshire couple on their way home from a vacation at Niagara Falls in 1961. They drove through Canada until they got to a border crossing in New Hampshire, at which point they still had a ways to go to reach home. Along the way, Betty saw a star that seemed to be moving, and pointed it out to Barney. It seemed to be getting bigger, and then they realized that it appeared to be getting closer to them. They made a stop along the way, and Barney got out and looked through his binoculars. He said it got close enough that he could see figures standing at a window watching them. He got back into the car, and they drove home. When they got home, they realized that it was a little later than they had expected, but they went to bed right after a quick breakfast, since it was very late into the night. When they awoke they could not concentrate on anything but the trip; however, they were unaware that they had been abducted. They just had many unanswerable questions of the event. Flashbacks and dreams bothered them till they met with Dr. Benjamin Simon and separate hypnotic regressions were conducted. The memories of their interrupted journey came out (*The Interrupted Journey* by John G. Fuller).

Karla Turner, PhD, was a teacher at a major university. She and her husband, who had been married once before, had a very good marriage with no concerns or problems. Karla noticed that her husband began having some "physical symptoms of stress," and she too was experiencing the anxiety. So they began going to separate sessions of counseling. On the return from a trip away from home with her husband, Karla noticed that he was having problems with back pains and numbness of his leg. Since Karla had been going to her counseling, she went through some hypnosis sessions and learned some relaxation techniques. She decided, with her husband's permission, to try some of these on him to find out what was causing him distress. What she discovered was to change her and her husband's lives forever. He suddenly started recalling being with his father at the age of two and seeing a UFO and its alien occupants (childhood initiation). Further sessions showed that he had numerous abductions throughout his life. She, over the next few months and years, would learn that not only had her husband been unwillingly and unknowingly having alien abduction experiences, but her son and she had been having them as well.

One particular experience to come out of the many hypnotically regressed memories was that of Karla's husband and her son going into what seemed like a tunnel into the ground, and there they remembered seeing men dressed in military uniforms. There were other people in the area also. The men in uniforms were not happy with her husband, since he apparently was not doing what he was supposed to be doing. Was this an alien abduction or was it a military abduction called a MILAB? Or is it possible that this was a combined alien and military abduction? There have been numerous reports by abductees of having been taken to an unknown place not seeming to be an alien craft, but more like an underground facility where both alien creatures and human military personnel have been reported. It is not known if the reported human personnel are truly human or a hybrid creation by the aliens.

In her book *How to Defend Yourself against Alien Abduction*, Ann Druffel tells the story of a Tennessee woman who had been having numerous abduction experiences and was working with UFO investigator Don Worley. The story tells how she and her husband had been having enough unwelcome experiences from these creatures that they moved their bedroom from a room in the back of their house to a room closer to the front. She had also learned that her two children were having nightly visitors. She was additionally pregnant with another child. One night they lay in bed and the woman noticed an unusual green light coming from the bathroom window into the bedroom. With that light was a recognizable humming sound that she remembered from previous abductions. When she looked toward the beam of light, she noticed three small Grey creatures walk out of the beam. Knowing what was about to happen, she suddenly developed an enormous amount of anger. She did not want to be abducted. Without thinking about it, and before she could have been put into a paralysis state (she thought the anger kept her from being paralyzed by them), she jumped out of bed and attacked her would-be abductors. She grabbed one of them by the neck, and, without trying, she squeezed a little too hard and snapped its neck. The other two creatures were shocked that she could do that, and that they weren't able to paralyze her. The creatures then picked up the body of their fallen comrade with what appeared to be a broken neck and disappeared back into the light. Abduction averted.

INFORMATION FROM ABDUCTION REPORTS GIVING MARKERS FOR PEOPLE WHO MAY HAVE EXPERIENCED AN ABDUCTION EVENT

AFTER READING THAT TITLE WITH A SOMEWHAT warped sense of humor, we envisioned the old *David Letterman Show* and the "Top Ten" skits he used to do. How about the top-ten signs that you may have been abducted?

10. Grey is not your favorite color.
9. Your frequent-flyer miles are mostly outside our atmosphere.
8. You think it's normal to see a UFO once a week.
7. The buzzing in your head makes the neighborhood dogs bark when you get near them.
6. You wake up with your neighbor's underwear on, and everybody wants to know why.
5. Your implant makes the metal detector at the county building go off. Being strip searched is getting old.
4. You got slivers from the last time you were abducted through the wall.
3. You have twenty-seven watches that all stopped at the same time.
2. Your car is so magnetic that all the tools in the garage are stuck to it.
1. Your next-door neighbors ask you to stop with the 3:00 a.m. light show with the 40-foot UFO lawn ornament.

If after reading that, and if you happen to be a person who has had strange occurrences or abduction events and you at least cracked a smile, there is hope for you. While we take this topic very seriously, humor does have its place. Humor has a healing effect on most of us, and we personally believe that it is one of the major things that gets us through the tough times. We've been around enough abductees to know it helps. In fact, we know some abductees who have great senses of humor, probably out of necessity, but nonetheless, flourishing.

During conferences and symposiums that we have attended over the years, in every case, there are always a couple of rooms in the hotel where all the abductees congregate and commiserate over experiences. The older abductees who have been aware of their experience for years take the new ones under their wing, console them, and let them know that they are not alone.

We have been an invited guest to some of these get-together events, and it is like a very warm and friendly family-like reunion. A group of people just like you and I, who in many cases have never met before, acting like long-lost friends and relatives. There is hugging and crying, but there is also laughter and good times. We have always considered it an honor to be included in such private times, and it is truly heartwarming to experience, and humor is a part of it.

It is our hope that no one takes offense at our lighthearted attempt at humor over a topic that can be heart wrenching to someone deep in the throes of discovery. We do indeed take it very seriously and mean no harm. Well, back to business on a more serious note.

"Can You Tell Me If I Have Been Abducted?"

We've heard it dozens of times, and we always cringe at its utterance. We as investigators and researchers personally avoid anything that has to do with answering a question like that. In other words, it is a question that we cannot and are not qualified to answer. Why? For one thing, the only one who truly knows is the person with the memories of an abduction event locked up inside their head and has gone through the personal investigation of their experience to unlock what they can to form their own opinion about it. Some researchers are qualified mental health professionals; most are not.

Number-one rule: Cause no harm. We can never be sure, positively, what happened to an individual coming to us for help and advice. Budd Hopkins once told me (Bob) in one of my visits to his Manhattan home that "I can't tell them if they have or haven't been abducted. Only they themselves with the experience can make that determination."

Whatever that answer is could certainly be a game changer for that person. Not everyone wants to know for sure, and in my opinion, not everyone should know if they are being or have been abducted. Some handle it very well. Some learn to cope and adapt, while some don't. One fellow we knew years ago said he would welcome the experience just so he could quiz his abductors and study them scientifically. We lovingly suspect that with this particularly very inquisitive individual that they would bring him back early and probably take his name off their list. Just my opinion; we could be wrong.

Another person, who shall remain nameless, once said to me (Bob), "I've never seen a UFO, and I wish one would just come and hover right over top of us so I could get a good look at it." I reminded him that if one were to be right over top of us, the chance of getting to see the *inside* of it would be very good. If he wanted to see the inside of the damn thing, fine; I, however, did NOT want to see the inside of one, and I begged him not to make wishes like that while I was standing next to him. (Note: He has since then seen a UFO. He can't remember if he saw the inside or not.)

So, the bottom line is this: Only the one who thinks that they may have had the abduction experience can make that call. Don't ask your researcher or investigator to make it for you.

Researchers and Investigators: Do not go down this road with the person you are trying to help investigate their experience. It's their call. It must be. There are abductee support groups out there that can help, and certified mental health professionals as well, if troubles and anxiety get too great to handle by yourself.

So, if someone suspects that they are having some type of anomalous event, what markers are there in abduction cases? They don't leave you a card reading "Thanks for coming; we'll be back for you on your next appointment, September 27." So how does one know?

When conducting an interview with a UFO witness, you don't want to jump to any conclusions as to whether he or she might be an abductee. And you definitely don't want to tell the witness that you may suspect they are. Learning that he or she may have been abducted and put through the trauma that some abductees go through can be very distressing. So, you need to look and listen for clues that they may tell you. In many instances, the witness does not know if he or she had been taken, and may not even want to know it. But, if asked the right questions, an experienced investigator can personally make a reasonable determination and allow that person being questioned to promote thought on the subject and perhaps come to their own conclusion. Remember, it's not an interrogation; it's a peaceful and friendly investigation.

We are not trying to teach investigators how to conduct an interview here, but to show anybody that there are certain clues that have indicated the possibility of an abduction event. Again, we stress only a possibility, not a definitive.

For the people who may not know if they have been abducted, if they are lucky they will never experience the flashbacks and anxiety so often associated with it. That statement may make it sound like it is better not to know. For some, that may be true. What typically gets done to an abductee during an abduction event, as we have already described in other chapters, is not a pleasant experience. Remember, it was a kidnapping. It is intrusive in nature. And this happens by nonhuman entities most of the time. If they offered milk and cookies, it would still not be a pleasant experience.

There are several telltale signs of abduction. Depending on your reference source, some groups use as few as five signs and some use as many as ten or more. There is no sure sign, and even if you have some or most of the signs of an abduction, it may be only a coincidence and not a sure thing. Many abductees have moments of normal unaided recall about abduction events anyway, making these markers only of significance for people with no memory but who have missing time or unexplainable, seemingly irrational fears.

When it comes to other unusual individual experiences, 1.4 percent, or 2.9 million Americans, say they have experienced at least four of five key events that believers of UFO abductions have identified as being of interest in examining whether UFO abductions might actually have taken place. Perhaps not surprisingly, those who believe in abductions and who have experienced, or know someone who experienced, a Close Encounter are more inclined to report an occurrence of at least four such events.

—Roper UFO poll in 2002

We believe that it takes more than four or five signs to suggest that an abduction event may have taken place. There probably isn't any set number, but here is a compilation of some of the more commonly accepted signs. Again, remember, this does not by any means confirm that a person has been abducted, only that further investigation is needed.

Scoop Marks, Body Scars, and Unusual Bleeding

Scars and scoop marks or missing chunks of skin are common if you were ever a teenage kid crashing bicycles, falling out of trees, or doing any number of stupid things that seemed like a good idea at the time but ended by going to the emergency room for stitches or worse.

Lots of people have scars. From my earlier days, the front of my legs looks like a flesh-colored road map of clumsy mayhem. Most often when something like that happens, you remember approximately, if not exactly, when it did happen. You have memories of it.

By the way, during any physical event where the body suffers trauma, adrenaline shoots into your system and makes your memories of the event even more ingrained. Stuff we did forty years ago is probably getting a little fuzzy, but, bottom line, you know most every inch of your body and how it got that way. If you discover something like an unexplainable scar or mark that seems to appear overnight, it still could mean nothing other than you don't remember how you did it.

Unexplainable scars and scoop marks began to crop up in people experiencing abduction events. A scoop mark is a small depression in the skin that may be found usually on the leg, arm, back, or neck, although they have been found on other places of the body as well. A scoop mark is very similar to a punch biopsy scar, for those who have ever experienced one. In other words, it's like someone took a small ice cream scoop and removed a small amount of flesh in the skin for examination. When one runs their finger over a scoop mark, there is an indentation in the skin that feels like a portion of muscle from under the skin is missing.

Body scars happen. Most all of us have a collection of scars from a wide range of sources. Again, most of us know exactly where and when we got them from. Bicycle wrecks, automobile accidents, normal surgeries, and everyday oops! that cause us to be scarred for life, so to speak. What we are talking about here are unexplainable scars.

The late Budd Hopkins worked with one fellow who woke one day with about a 5-inch scar in the center of his back, over his spine. It was healed, but he had absolutely no idea where it came from. As I recall the story, he went to his doctor to be examined, and his doctor asked him when he had had the back surgery. He replied that he had not ever had back surgery. A little perturbed with the man's answer, the doctor then asked him why he had a back-surgery scar over his spine. It was almost as if he thought the man was lying to him about his surgery. He wasn't.

I (Bob) also remember Budd saying that a debunker tried to say that the wound was self-inflicted, but, of course, Budd pointed out that the man could not even reach the center of his spine with his hands, to which the debunker said that the man must have mounted a knife to the wall and backed into it . . . I don't mind healthy skepticism, but you have to love some of the debunkers. Anything is possible except an abduction by nonhuman entities, in their eyes.

I had a case where a woman I was working with had a long history of female-related issues. She had numerous miscarriages and had been diagnosed with missing-fetus syndrome as well. I ask how many miscarriages she'd had, and her reply was thirteen! She had been confirmed pregnant many times, but the baby never developed much past the first trimester, around the twelve-to-sixteen-week period. No fetus was ever recovered from the so-called miscarriages. A couple of times she was told that she suffered from missing-fetus syndrome, and that the fetus had been absorbed by the body. It was present on ultrasounds, and then it was not there. Later on, she had to have a complete hysterectomy, and the doctor commented on her ovarian tubes. He said that they were so badly scarred up, he thought she had already had a tubal litigation, and had no idea how she could have ever gotten pregnant in the first place, let alone having done it thirteen times.

Abduction literature is loaded with cases of women being implanted with a modified fetus for them to carry for a short time, and then they are abducted again to have it removed and whisked away. We won't go into any more details in regard to that at this time, but it is out there, and if we are talking about an alien control issue, how much more personal could you be than having a fetus implanted without choice into your body and then having it removed at a later date—no different than harvesting a crop.

A number of abductees report waking up in the morning with dried drops of blood on their pillow. First and foremost, a nasal bleed can be caused by several reasons that have nothing to do with an abduction event and are not too hard to explain away. In some cases, very high blood pressure can rupture nasal arteries. Allergies can affect the sinus membranes, and irritating pollen in the area can be a factor. Lack of atmospheric moisture can cause drying and cracking of the nasal membranes. Some children are even known to stick things up their nose and accidentally make them bleed. Some sinus decongestants used too much can affect the membranes in the nose and make them thin and easy to rupture.

The nasal bleeding that we are talking about often has a memory that goes along with it. We would like to cite a case in Manhattan, New York, of a family of four. There were five people in a high-rise apartment: two young brothers, another child who was staying the night, and the mother and father. They all woke up at 4:20 a.m. with serious nosebleeds of the right nostril. Two of the five consciously remembered parts of their abduction experience, and all five remember waking up on their backs, choking on blood running down their throats, and then all walking to the bathroom for something to stop the bleeding, with all bumping into each other on the way. Picture the bizarre nature of the moment as all five people sit around the living room, holding their noses with toilet tissue to make them stop bleeding, all at 4:20 in the morning. These nosebleeds are caused by a procedure involving a nasal implant being inserted and lodged up the sinus cavity. Some abductees remember a small, rod-like mechanical device inserted into the nose. On the end are fingers holding what looks to be a small BB-sized ball. It is inserted to the point of one feeling a painful sensation and hearing a crunching sound, then the rod is removed and the BB is no longer on the end of the rod. Abductees have reported that they feel that their brain was actually penetrated in this procedure, making it a scary event! Some report problems with a diminished sense of smell as well, presumably linked to such a procedure affecting the olfactory bulb area, high in the nasal cavity and located close to the brain, just on the other side of the cribriform plate, separating the cranial vault. The olfactory nerve has a short, direct path to the brain and conceivably could serve as a place to implant a device either to monitor brain activity or *control* brain activity or function. It makes sense that such a short, direct path could be used for some type of mind control.

There have been a few reports of abductees feeling as if a hole is being drilled into the back of their head. They feel pressure and then a wet, warm feeling, followed by it getting hotter and the smell of something burning. A red spot about the size of a quarter has been found in the area of the sensation. A 32-year-old waitress and mother of three reported having dried blood on her scalp at least five times, with sensitive areas behind her ears on both sides of the head.

Bleeding from the ear may be caused by a ruptured eardrum or an unnoticed itch or scratch. It may have been something that happened some time ago and scabbed over or was covered with ear wax. However, many people experiencing an event have reported unexplained bleeding from the ear. Many report during an abduction event a procedure that causes pain to come from one or both ears, and the feeling of something hot and maybe needle- or laser-like being put into the ear. Again, if one can control brain function, one can control the individual. The best way to gain access to the brain is a hole in the head. In Whitley Strieber's book *Communion*, he remembered the aliens inserting a needle into his head, and he was terrified and tried to tell his captors that it would hurt or damage or even kill him. A very rational fear for anyone.

Flashbacks

Flashbacks are bits and pieces of a lost or misplaced memory trying to come back into focus in your head. It may be nothing more than the result of trying to remember someone's name after you finished trying unsuccessfully to remember it. And that flashback of a memory can go away again just as fast as it came. Some abductees have reported seeing a very brief, fleeting image of an unusual being such as a Grey. They may remember lying on a hospital bed when they hadn't done so in a long time. It might be seeing a light in the dark sky. Whatever the image is, it is usually brief but may come back a few times, and each time it may last a little longer.

A flashback doesn't always mean that a missing memory of an alien abduction is trying to make a comeback. It may be a memory of some other type of traumatic experience that happened and was self-forgotten by the person, such as a violent physical or sexual abuse by some person in the past. In fact, some investigated purported cases of abduction turned out to be something totally different, such as sexual abuse buried from long ago that came out during hypnotic regression. Sometimes hypnotherapists get exactly what they think they will get, and sometimes, something totally out of left field shows up. I'm sure there have been cases of a therapist working with what they believed to be a case of repressed sexual assault or abuse to suddenly have their patient start describing a nonhuman attacker and a very unexpected abduction event! Some therapists have developed specialized skills and work with many abductees, after having become familiar with this extremely unusual scenario; for other therapists, it may be their first trip down the rabbit hole for this type of anomalous event, being totally unfamiliar with this experience and with no baseline to judge it from, and they may not know where to turn.

In either case, a flashback may have been the starting point for an investigation to begin with. We have had people contact us over the years due to a flashback of something strange or disturbing, and then they start to look online and find the myriad information (both good and bad, and sometimes incorrect) and look for someone to help them sort it all out. Flashback-perceived memories and sometimes the trigger-point events that cause the flashbacks are responsible for most of the information that we have today coming to light in the first place. A flashback is usually perceived as a burst of memory, but what about a flashback memory of a dream? Meaning the memory is real but the content of the memory is not. This is where you get into dream or memory interpretation.

Déjà Vu

Déjà vu, premonitions, or precognition. How many times have we seen something or someone, and we know we have seen them or experienced the circumstance before but cannot recall any instance of it? Have you ever met someone and said, "Have we met before?" Or while going someplace, have you thought that everything seemed familiar but you don't remember ever being there before?

These flashes are fairly commonplace, and most have nothing to do with a possible abduction event. One thing to remember is that we are made from elements from the periodic table. These elements are mixed with the water that makes up about 75 percent of our body weight. The elements are joined together to form chemical compounds and, ultimately, life, which is us. If you break us down to our most basic form, our stored memories are made of chemicals, which reduced to their base are molecules. So, thoughts and memories are stored as molecules.

The human body is a constant changing mass of molecules. Cells are continually being replaced with new ones, while old ones are broken down and expelled from the body. A constant renewing as we take in new molecules of food to become new building blocks to our body and our memory. So, what complicates memory is that it is molecularly being rebuilt with new molecules as cells die and are replaced. The cells that we have right now that contain our memories are not the same cells we had a year ago, essentially, and that goes for the memories contained chemically within those cells.

Before you start to doubt the validity of your memories, think about this. Your body replicates exact replicas of trillions of cells yearly. Each cell had a DNA blueprint of you in it. You are still you, after several complete cellular changeovers though the years—and so are your memories. However, memories, as we all know, seem to dull with time. We believe that this is due to the memories being rebuilt time and time again on a cellular basis, without a refresher backup. The food you eat affects your memory and brain. The drugs you ingest affect your memory and brain. The stress of your environment and the hormones you produce affect your memory and brain. After all, your memories are just chemicals consisting of bonded atoms.

So, we have established that you are one big, walking, talking chemical soup that is always in flux of being torn down and rebuilt, including your memories. Miraculous to say the least. We mentioned a refresher backup to your memory. What is this? Just anytime you use your memory to think back. The more often you recall a memory, the less degradation that seems to occur in that memory. A picture album is a tremendous backup system, just like backing up your hard drive on your computer. When you see a fresh picture of a memory frozen in time, just as it was, that memory is refreshed in your brain to a sharper image. How many times has someone said to you, "Do you remember so and so?," and while you have not thought about that person or thing in years, memories come flooding back, and the more input you get from that person asking the question, the more you seem to remember, which was just lost somewhere beforehand.

Hormones affect memories too. If during a traumatic experience you become excited enough to have your adrenal gland give you a shot of adrenaline, your memories during that time seem to be recalled easier and in higher definition. It's the body's way of saying that you should definitely remember this traumatic experience so that you can avoid it next time and live through it.

Our point in all of this is that sometimes the feeling of déjà vu is the recalling of a memory that is very similar in experience to what you are experiencing at the moment you are thinking "déjà vu" but, due to becoming "fuzzy" over time, is being pulled from a much-broader spectrum of memory and seems similar enough to be recalled as that exact experience. Please understand that we are not discounting precognitive events here, just briefly explaining the memory process to differentiate between the two.

Two abductees, Anna Jamerson and Beth Collings, as children, had numerous abductions from different locations and were put together by the aliens aboard the alien craft. They did not know each other in normal life and did not live near each other. Yet, many years later they were drawn together when Anna pulled into Beth's horse farm looking for a job. During conversation between the two, they began realizing some sense of déjà vu. Beth described a childhood memory of seeing a girl who was wearing a school uniform with a school emblem from a British school. Anna said that she was a student in a British school and wore a school uniform.

In the book *Witnessed*, by Budd Hopkins, he tells the story of a woman named Linda Cortile who was taken from her apartment building near the Brooklyn Bridge. The book concentrates mostly on the witnesses of the incident as well as the abduction itself. One of the witnesses was a political person who was being escorted by bodyguards from the NYPD. These witnesses were discovered to have been abducted as well. In an attempt to learn more about what happened, the two officers tried to find the woman they saw being lifted from her apartment in a beam of light along with smaller alien-looking beings. During an interview with Linda, one of the officers realized that there was something familiar about her. Linda had the same feelings. It was determined that the two had been abducted and put together during alien abduction encounters for many years.

Total Recall

Total recall of abduction events is not unheard of by abductees. Most, at least initially, are returned with no recall of the event, but some have been able to be conscious and aware of the events as they happened and even after being returned. It is not completely clear why this occurs—maybe it is a brain-wiring issue, and the aliens cannot cause the memories to be blocked or erased. It may even be a trust issue, that the person is so controlled that being able to remember isn't considered to be a problem and may even aid in future abduction events by lessening the trauma with the memories of "Oh, this has happened before and I came back okay."

Unidentified Flying Objects

UFO reports are common. Many people see things in the sky that they cannot identify. Both of us, having been investigators with MUFON, have learned quickly that 95 percent of all UFO reports are completely identifiable to the trained investigator as atmospheric events or astronomical event, or involving mechanical craft that are very much from the Planet Earth. While sighting reports are common, having someone see something in the sky that they cannot identify is often a once-in-a-lifetime event for that person.

Having said that, numerous UFO sightings by one person are not a common occurrence. Most people will go their entire life without seeing a UFO or remembering seeing one, as in the case of some abductees. However, there are many people who seem to see UFOs a lot more often than they probably want to. No matter where they live at the time, they see what appears to be an unidentified flying object. Moving many miles away from where they see them a lot, such as from their home, they can still see them where they move to. Is it because they think every object is a UFO, or could it be because they are being tracked and followed? Do the beings inside a UFO allow certain people to see them and not others? This question is addressed in chapter 12, discussing why some people can see UFOs and others can't.

Implants

Finding an anomalous object implanted somewhere in the body might be another indication. This subject is addressed further in chapter 10, about implants. However, finding something stuck somewhere in the skin doesn't necessarily mean that it is an alien implant. The work of people such as Dr. Roger Leir, Derrel Simms, Steve Colbern, and others has made a great deal of progress in the discovery of implants, removing them, and analyzing them. An alien implant is nothing like a sliver, and when it is removed and analyzed, the possibility of someone having been abducted becomes almost a certainty.

Family History

Having a family history of UFO sightings and abductions is another good indication that you may have been abducted. Genetics plays a big role in who might get abducted at one time or another. One of the scariest aspects of being abducted isn't what happened to the abductee, but learning that they have been abducted since almost birth, and that there is a high possibility that their children are going to go through the same thing. Whether the aliens are following the genetic family lines to learn of human development and progress, it is almost certain that children who are abducted grow up to become parents and have children who are being abducted too.

Pregnancy Discrepancies

Being unexplainably pregnant and then being unexplainably not pregnant is a mix of mystery, joy, and sorrow. Learning that a woman is pregnant can be one of the greatest joys she can go through. However, becoming pregnant after an alien abduction is going to cause a lot of grief, anger, and disappointment, especially if there is no explanation for the sudden pregnancy for family and friends to understand. In some cases, there is no male counterpart in the woman's life at that time for it to happen. How does she explain it? If it is an alien-induced pregnancy, she is going to lose the baby within a few months and will have no idea why she isn't pregnant anymore. This is not indicating that the baby is dead; it is presumed that the embryo had been removed by the aliens to grow up in their environment. Usually the woman is abducted later to allow her to hold and show affection toward the baby or small child, who she is told is hers, or, more often than not, she feels a distinctive bond with the child and knows intuitively that it is hers.

But don't assume that just because a woman gets pregnant and loses the baby that it had to be alien caused. Life happens, and there must be a long history of involvement with this phenomenon before someone might consider that scenario.

A Feeling of Being Watched

A feeling of being watched and or communicated with can make a person think that he or she is going crazy. Some people hear voices in their head and some don't. Usually it is just their imaginations or their subconscious talking; it's the same with thinking that you are constantly being watched. With all the cameras set up in buildings and along the roadways, it is almost impossible not to feel as though you are being watched—because you are. When you are in your own home, you should be able to feel confident that you are not being watched, but some people still do.

Are they monitoring abductees? Implants would be the easiest way to know *where* anybody would be. In the old science fiction TV shows, space beings would watch people from a monitor in their craft. Could they be able to do that? Or are we just getting paranoid?

Let's examine some of the well-known abduction cases and consider how the subjects knew they were abducted.

Antonio Villa Boas was abducted in 1956 while working on a farm driving a tractor, when he noticed an object coming toward him and then was abducted. Boas remembered seeing the craft approaching him before his abduction and had total recall of all the events during and after. He said that while on the craft, his clothes had been removed, he was covered with some kind of clear liquid gel, and then he was put into a room, where he came across what he thought was a beautiful blond woman who began to caress him, and then they made love twice. His only complaint was that during the lovemaking, she would howl like a dog. Boas was able to recount his experience as soon as it was over, but did not reveal it for many years (John Spencer, *The UFO Encyclopedia* [1993]).

Betty and Barney Hill had their abduction while driving home at night from a vacation in Niagara Falls, on their way home to New Hampshire in 1961. When they got home that night, they discovered that they had arrived home much later than they should have. Soon they began having strange dreams and flashbacks and couldn't explain unusual marks on their bodies. They sought help and met with a psychiatrist, undergoing regressive hypnosis to determine what was bothering them, and that drew out the experience.

When Frank Soriano, in 1998, videotaped his UFO sighting in Ticonderoga, he did not realize that the same object had circled around and come back to abduct him. All he was able to remember was that he seemed to lose the enthusiasm for recording the UFO and put his camera away; he never discussed or even thought to discuss the sighting or recording with his wife for eight days. When I (Jim) interviewed him and asked him what he did after the incident, he could not remember. Although I thought he was abducted, I did not feel it was the right time to tell him. I decided to wait until I thought he could handle the knowledge. Frank would constantly call me up and complain that he would wake up in the middle of the night wondering what happened, or tell me about some very brief flashback that he had; we discussed the possibility of an alien abduction. After about four years, Frank met with world-renowned abduction researcher Budd Hopkins and went through a session of hypnotic regression where he realized all that happened, and he was at peace with it all. The weight had been lifted off his shoulders and his mind was at rest, having the ability to deal with the circumstances now that he knew, consciously, what had happened.

In November 1993, Frank Soriano and his wife, Miriam, were driving home from work after midnight in a heavy rainstorm when they saw a large, bright light sitting over a mountain. They had driven this road hundreds of times going to and from work and knew that the mountain had nothing but trees on it. There were no structures and no roads on the mountain. As they got closer, they could see it better, although it was raining at the time. They pulled over and stared at the lighted object. The Sorianos described it as two railroad cars, one on top of the other. It was about a mile long, and the windows on the object were two rows of large lights. They had watched the lighted object for only a few minutes when Miriam told Frank that it was time to go. Frank wanted to see it a little longer and had his head out the window in the rain to get a better view. Miriam insisted that they go and leave immediately. Frank was still wrapped up in watching the object and didn't want to leave yet. Miriam got louder in her insistence to go and started yelling at Frank. She insisted that they had to go, that they weren't supposed to see this, that they were being watched, and that *they had to go*. Frank hesitated a bit longer and Miriam got vocal and began hitting Frank, telling him to get them out of there. They did not realize that there may have been any kind of abduction until they met with Budd Hopkins.

Miriam refused to discuss what happened for a long time, and when she accompanied Frank to meet with Hopkins, Frank mentioned the incident, and Budd asked Miriam about it. She mentioned the very same thing to Budd that Frank had, except she insisted that there were many more lights than Frank described. Miriam said that there were many smaller lights around the bigger lights. Frank disagreed with her, saying that he did not see any other lights, and he had had his head out of the window for a better view. Budd, realizing the discrepancy, suggested that Miriam saw the other lights better than he did because she had been closer. Frank said that she had been with him the whole time, and they had watched it only a few minutes. Miriam began to realize then that her fears were true, that she had seen it from a closer distance and that she had been abducted. In further discussions she began to remember (without hypnosis) seeing large Greys near the object (investigations by Jim Bouck).

08

CONTROL

How Are We Controlled by Our Own Fellow Humans?

Throughout the ages, the power struggle to maintain control over one's life has always been present. In medieval times of England, the hierarchy of kings and dukes, squires and lords, and the common man and slaves was the accepted level of control. Similar were the plantation owners and slaves in the beginning of America's history.

Responsible parents control or attempt to control the activities of their children, up to the point that they can take responsible control of themselves. Our government makes laws to control the actions of the people to keep us safe and obedient to the laws. Schools and teachers control what we learn, and control our development toward being educated.

People can now control their surroundings by the push of a button or voice activation. Radios, televisions, car starters, toys, and the lights and temperature of your house when you're not at home can be controlled by the use of a smartphone or computer. The human race has strived for more and more finely tuned control of everything in their lives. Let's take a more in-depth look at the term "control" and what it means.

"Control" on a mechanical level can be as simple as to make something turn off or turn on. "Control" on a personal level gives the controller the ability to allow or forbid the personal decision-making control of another. It can be to make someone act in a way that they wouldn't normally act on their own. Sometimes personal control is manipulated by another without the intended victim being aware, using trickery, deceit, and confusion. Almost anybody can be fooled and manipulated to some extent.

> If you can control the meaning of words, suspend critical judgment, and appeal to the mechanistic drive, you can control the masses. These are the basic tools of the manipulator.
>
> —Eldon Taylor, *Mind Programming*

How much control one is under depends on the effort and sometimes the technology put forth by the controller. Remember, we are all preprogrammed even before we are born by information stored in our DNA. Our genetic mind comes from our parents and their parents, and we emulate what we see and experience as we mature to adults. Our history, culture, and even politics set in motion what we are being taught. At adulthood, when we can think for ourselves and make our own decisions, we determine whether to continue the path that we were taught, or how we were raised, or the path we were expected to follow, or we make a life-altering change embracing a different direction or behavior.

Wherever we go and whatever we do, we are going to have to deal with those who want us to do something differently than we normally would have. Just look at television. How many commercials tell us what car to buy, which one is the best—and how many times do we see it being replayed again and again? Advertisers are the biggest villains of mind control.

Subliminal messages are all around us, but we fail to notice them because they are hidden so well. These messages are designed to pass below the normal limits of perception. An inaudible message, if you will, to the conscious mind but completely audible to the deeper unconscious mind, usually an image transmitted briefly, unperceived consciously, yet perceived unconsciously. You could be quite content to sit and watch a ball game on television, when suddenly the need for a beer, soda, or something to eat hits, and you jump up and head to the refrigerator. It could have been your stomach telling you to do that . . . or was it your brain?

Another example of mass mind control occurs every year before November. Elections bring out the worst in attempts to control what you believe. No matter what your inclination is before the campaigns begin, someone is going to try to make you think the way they want you to. Their candidate is the one they want you to vote for, and they will attempt to persuade your decision in such a way that every time you think you've made up your mind, you will have to rethink your choices. (Now if only someone could come up with a foolproof way to control the dog not to chew your shoes or furniture, or a cat not to scratch everything in sight when you're not looking.)

How far one can control another person depends on several factors, such as the susceptibility of the targeted person. To get someone to buy a particular brand of automobiles is a little different than getting someone to rob a bank or kill someone.

We know now that men can be made to do exactly anything . . . It's all a question of finding the right means. If only we take enough trouble and go sufficiently slowly, we can make him kill his aged parents and eat them in a stew.

—Jules Romain, from a CIA handbook on brainwashing

Human Control by Government Entities

Depending on where you live and the customs of your country, the government might be the major force of control. If you live in a democracy, there is some but not too much constant control over your lives. There are laws to obey and penalties for not doing so, but you enjoy a great deal of freedom. If you live in a socialistic country, there are some freedoms to enjoy, but the government seems to put a lot of conditions on you and rules that need to be followed. The government also does much more for you, so you don't have to worry if you should do this or do that; they tell you what to do. If you live in a dictatorship or a communist country, you have little or no freedom other than what you are told to do; they will provide for you everything they think you need. In the United States in 1863, during his delivery of the Gettysburg Address, Abraham Lincoln stated that we have "a government of the people, by the people and for the people." The government is here to serve the people of this great country. Today, some would suggest that the government is now your controller. Your very existence and the freedoms you still get to enjoy are at the whim of the government leaders, especially since the power of the executive order has started coloring outside the framework of our Constitution here in the United States.

Governments are broken down into finer points in that you are subjected to rules and laws of states and cities or townships. Each has its chain of order. Here in the United States, we are governed by the federal government, made up of three major branches: the executive, the legislative, and the judicial. Each branch has its own authority, and each is to make sure that neither of the other two exceed their constitutional authority, therefore supposedly having effective checks and balances.

A portion of the executive branch is that of National Intelligence, which is overseen by the director of National Intelligence (DNI). One of the agencies under the command of the DNI is the Central Intelligence Agency (CIA). Under the provisions of the National Security Act of 1947 (the same year as the alleged Roswell saucer crash), the National Security Council (NSC) and the CIA were created. When the CIA was first organized, it was responsible only to the president of the United States. Now it is buried with many other newer divisions of intelligence and defense agencies, all under the auspices of the DNI, and has become a labyrinth of information sectioning and divvies out information on a need-to-know basis. It is theorized that very few have a complete picture about anything covered under the auspice of national security, resulting in complete control of information.

The United States has taken a very big interest in other countries' control techniques, especially the old Soviet Union and Nazi Germany. Since this book is basically about UFOs and their ability to control some of our earthly systems and certain people as well, naturally other controlling countries had an interest in them also.

The UFO phenomenon is shared by every country on the planet, and its inherent technology would create a severe imbalance in the wrong hands.

According to the International UFO Museum and Research Center in Roswell, New Mexico, in 1937, as Nazi Germany was rising to power, an incredible thing happened: A distressed UFO crashed into German territory (*Secret Treaty: The United States Government and Extra-terrestrial Entities* by Richard K. Wilson and Sylvan Burns). The German army was there to take possession of the crashed craft. No record was ever found suggesting whether any bodies were retrieved from the alleged crash site. Upon receiving information of the crash, Adolf Hitler immediately ordered elements of the Luftwaffe and Germany's top aeronautical experts to examine the remains of the craft.

The heavily damaged disc was moved to a heavily guarded warehouse near the Rhine River. From there, pieces were moved to other secret locations for further scrutiny. Allegedly, a team of university professors and industrial engineers, along with members of the Luftwaffe and the Speer Ministry of Arms, worked to unlock the secrets of the advanced alien technology. The object here was to reverse engineer what was salvaged from the crashed saucer and to see how it could benefit the Nazis' war efforts. Many experts and engineers were called in, including the Horten brothers, who were German aircraft enthusiasts and pilots. Although they had little, if any, formal engineering training in the field of aeronautics, the Hortens designed some of the most advanced aircraft of World War II, including the world's first jet-powered flying wing, the Horten Ho 229, which was also to be the first stealth jet fighter-bomber for the Nazis. Was the technology gleaned from the alien craft? No one knows for sure.

Italian researcher Renato Vesco, in his classic and well-researched book *Intercept—but Don't Shoot: The True Story of the Flying Saucers* (2018), asserts that the Nazis were working on many advanced propulsion systems and rudimentary antigravity devices to power their disc-shaped, or lenticular, aircraft.

The crashed craft pushed advancements in propulsion and electronics and provided clues to workable designs, but the scientists were still at a loss, not unlike a four-year-old child trying to reverse engineer a smartphone—much to the good luck of the Allied forces in Europe and the rest of the world, for that matter. Had they unraveled that technology to a greater degree, we would all probably be speaking German. Hitler knew that technology so advanced would allow him to remain in control and take over the world. He had personally tasked some of Germany's mostly advanced theoretical engineers and physicists to get the alien technology working and apply it to the war efforts. In that regard, geniuses such as Giuseppe Belluzzo, Otto Habermohl, Dr. Richard Miethe, and Rudolf Schriever were recruited. Fortunately, US and Allied forces put an end to the Nazi development of the alien technology before it was too late.

The Allied forces captured documents after the war that indicated that Rudolf Schriever was the first to have some success with the disc technology. His own research, augmented by what had been deduced from the retrieved saucer, enabled him to build a working craft powered by specially designed jet engines. The craft, however, was unstable. The first two versions ended in disastrous crashes, killing the test pilots (David Hatcher Childress, *Man-Made UFOs, 1944–1994: Fifty Years of Suppression* [1995]).

The best known of saucer projects is referred to as the Schriever-Habermohl project. Otto Habermohl and Rudolf Schriever were the engineers who headed the project, centered at the PragGbell airport in Prag. Joseph Andreas Epp, also an engineer, had the advantage of being a consultant not only on the Schriever-Habermohl project, but also the Miethe-Belluzzo disc projects. Miethe was an Italian engineer and Belluzzo was a senior scientist under Mussolini. Epp stated that fifteen disc prototypes in total were built, since he was connected to all disc-related projects.

At this point, the war was going poorly, and the Russian army was becoming a threat to the PragGbell airport. Chaos ensued; the technicians working on these projects started to scurry like rats on a sinking ship. They looted the facility of anything of value, and all the disc prototypes were pushed onto the tarmac and set on fire.

Habermohl had gone missing and was thought to be captured by the Soviets. Schriever was reported to have died in 1953. This was shortly after he was approached by other governments looking to glean any of his knowledge of the disc project. Supposedly, he popped up again, alive and well in Bavaria in the early '60s, being seen by someone who knew him, suggesting that maybe he did do some postwar work on flying discs for some otherworldly entity. He may have been scooped up under Operation Paperclip along with so many of the German scientists.

The US government has been working on mind control techniques for over a half century, and it all began just after World War II. In 1945, the CIA was able to bring German scientists into the country to help them with special projects, even though they were admitted Nazi scientists. This program was called "Operation Paperclip," which was a secret program to expunge their Nazi memberships and provide them with false employment and political biographies. Operation Paperclip moved over 1,500 German scientists, technicians, and engineers to US soil and offered citizenship. One of the better-known Nazi scientists was Wernher von Braun, who worked in Germany's rocket development program, where he helped design and develop the V-2 rocket that bombed Britain during World War II. He was a member of the Nazi Party and the notorious SS. Later, Von Braun became an American aerospace engineer and is credited with the development of the Saturn V rocket for the Apollo moon missions.

As a side note here before we get too far off the mark, Wernher von Braun and another German scientist, Dr. Hermann Oberth, while both having worked on the Nazi V-2 rockets at the German Peenemunde Army Research Center, as well as the designs for the Saturn V rocket in the US space program, may have had something to do with a Nazi attempt to develop a levitating disk. Nazis had a fascination with UFOs, and rumors of creating a Nazi-designed disk were floated about. Both Oberth and Von Braun made statements of a very strange nature in years after the fall of Nazi Germany.

"We cannot take credit for our record advancement in certain scientific fields alone. We have been helped." When asked by whom, he replied, "the peoples of other worlds."

Dr. Hermann Oberth: "We find ourselves faced by powers, which are far stronger than we had hitherto assumed, and whose base is at present unknown to us. More I cannot say at present. We are now engaged in entering into closer contact with those powers, and in six or nine months it may be possible to speak with some precision on the matter."

After the Allied capture of Peenemunde Army Research Center, the US discovered exactly how far the Nazi scientists were ahead of anything that we were working on. Did the Nazis somehow have "help" from outside this world? And if so, was that a major part of the decision for the enactment of "Operation Paperclip"—to ensure that this technology became US property along with the Germans and Nazis who were working on it, and not fall into the hands of the Soviet Union after the crumbling of the Nazi empire?

Nazi interest did not end with rocket and weapon technology. Prior to the twentieth century, Germans had immersed themselves into psychology and psychiatry with an application to warfare in mind, even to the extent of exploring exotic sciences and occult practices. Not all the scientists brought in by Operation Paperclip were rocket scientists or engineers. Some of these so-called scientists were war criminals and had studied various methods of torture and brainwashing.

Operation Paperclip was the precursor to what became known as MKULTRA. According to Richard Dolan, in his book *UFOs and the National Security State*, "Several secret US government projects grew out of Operation Paperclip. These projects included Project Chatter (est. in 1947), and Project Bluebird (est. in 1950). Which was renamed Project Artichoke in 1951. Their purpose was to study mind control interrogation, behavior modification and related topics."

Dr. Sidney Gottlieb and Project MKULTRA

In 1951, Gottlieb joined the Central Intelligence Agency. As a poison expert, he headed the chemical division of the Technical Services Staff (TSS). Gottlieb became known as the "Black Sorcerer" and the "Dirty Trickster." He supervised preparations of lethal poisons and experiments in mind control.

MKULTRA ran from 1953 through 1973. Dr. Gottlieb worked under the direction of CIA director Allen Dulles and spearheaded Project MKULTRA, which tested LSD and other mind-altering drugs on unwitting suspects.

Gottlieb also constructed various scenarios to assassinate leaders unfriendly to the United States by using mind control, including plans to kill Fidel Castro at the time.

Most of the subjects—or should we say victims—of the MKULTRA experiments were never consulted, and the experiments were conducted without their knowledge or permission. The CIA's choice of drug for these experiments was LSD. Many of the experiments using LSD and other drugs were done to CIA employees, military personnel, doctors, and other government agents. Along with the drugs, hypnosis was used in many cases to reinforce the amount of control.

Although there may have been many deaths because of these illegal and dangerous experiments, only one death was attributed to it: Frank Olson, a biochemist for the US Army and biological weapons researcher, was given LSD in 1953 without his knowledge or consent, although the CIA insists that Olson was aware prior to the drug experiment.

Supposedly, Olson was put into a hotel room and was under the supervision of a doctor after the drug was introduced. The doctor claims to have been asleep in another bedroom in the hotel when Olson allegedly climbed out of a window on the fourteenth floor and fell to his death. Olson's family insists that he was murdered because he had recently quit his job due to moral objections to experiments being done and the purpose behind them.

Reports vary that he was depressed and jumped out a window during a psychotic break, or that the CIA, which felt he was a security risk and might reveal details of the program, murdered him.

On a side note, this sounds extremely familiar to the death of James Forrestal, the first US secretary of defense and an alleged member of MJ-12, the secret group that handled the Roswell crash of a UFO. President Truman made the decision to dismiss him as secretary of defense on March 31, 1949, after Forrestal was found to be making plans with one of Truman's rivals for the office of the president. It is said to have caused him to have a "nervous breakdown," a charge that was always denied by Forrestal's brother.

Forrestal was hospitalized on April 2, 1949. On May 22, 1949, he was found dead on the roof of a covered walkway below the window of a kitchen across the hall from his sixteenth-floor room at the National Naval Medical Center (NNMC, commonly known as the Bethesda Naval Hospital), a bathrobe sash knotted tightly around his neck. This happened on the day Forrestal was to be discharged from the hospital.

Why would someone who was ready to be released from a hospital, who had been suffering reportedly from depression but was better, tie a robe sash around his neck to strangulate himself and then throw himself out a window?

Maybe he was depressed. Maybe he wasn't. Maybe Forrestal just wasn't going to be controlled in the normal fashion. Maybe someone strangled him and then threw his body out a sixteen-story window to cover it up. But hey, that's just our opinion; maybe we're wrong.

Either way, there seems to be a pattern of government employees who worked in highly secretive projects but wanted out of their assigned project on moral grounds suddenly getting depressed and possibly being helped out of fourteen-to-sixteen-story windows, to the ground.

When the knowledge of what was happening started to leak out, MKULTRA was eventually, *officially*, scrapped, and all documents were thought to be destroyed to prevent repercussions from the public and other government agencies. Instead, many of the experiments, although still under the funding of the CIA, were moved to Canada. When word of this eventually came out, it was learned also that the Canadian government had known of this and was even funding it themselves.

Another means of mind control that the government is accused of participating in is called MILABS—or Military Abductions. As mentioned earlier, there have been numerous cases in which an abductee recalled seeing not just an alien presence but that of a human-looking figure in a military uniform. Could our government or some other government be in collusion with alien entities? Or do the aliens have a hybrid program so advanced at this stage that they are mistaken for humans? (Technically they are part human, although we don't really know how much, other than looks.) The hybrid program has been going forward for decades, as is covered in the latest book by Dr. David Jacobs, *Walking Among Us: The Alien Plan to Control Humanity* (2015). Earlier in the book we talked about the collection of ova and sperm during the abductions, and the creation of hybrid children that has advanced to the point of having adult hybrids who reportedly look totally human but are primarily alien mentally and can mentally control humans, but on a lesser level than the Greys.

One instance of an abduction with military presence is that of a woman named Lisa, who was an abductee who started out working with researcher Dr. Karla Turner. When Dr. Turner (author of *Taken: Inside the Alien-Human Abduction Agenda* [2013]), who had many abductions (including with military and alien presence), passed away, Lisa began working with Kay Wilson. Wilson has been a member of MUFON for over twenty years, having served as a MUFON investigator and a state section director in the Northwest. Kay Wilson also has had the same type of experiences.

In one of her many papers on the subject, titled "MILABS: Project Open Mind," Kay Wilson tells of Lisa's experiences. Lisa was a young wife and mother when she spoke of the abductions. Lisa had had many abduction experiences, not all with aliens, but some by our military or what was perceived to be our military. Besides the abductions, Lisa has reported a constant presence of military planes and helicopters flying over her house and neighborhood. She recalls that when she was abducted by alien entities, she found herself in a white, round room. During her military abductions, she found herself on a medical examining table in a really small, white-brick-walled room.

Her military abductions usually began by hearing a Morse Code–like sound followed by an intermittent humming sound. Many alien abductees report that prior to their abduction, there is a clicking sound. Lisa reports that numerous times during an abduction, she has experienced incidents of abuse and rape by nonalien military-dressed personnel. She has been threatened, as have her husband and other family members.

Lisa believes that they have been attempting to program her. She thinks they want her to kill someone. In her paper, Wilson goes into much detail on Lisa's experiences. As of this writing, it is not known if Lisa has been subjected to any more abductions and programming.

In their book *MILABS: Military Mind Control and Alien Abductions* (2000), Dr. Helmut and Marion Lammer write about a woman named Michelle (a pseudonym).

Michelle and her boyfriend were visiting one of her relatives in Montauk, New York, on Long Island, when they experienced some missing time. Concerned about this, Michelle had a session of regressive hypnosis to see if she could learn anything about it. What she learned was that she and her boyfriend were abducted by men dressed in military uniforms and taken to an underground facility in Montauk. There, Michelle was placed on a table and was unable to move. When the soldiers left the room, a tall, reptilian-looking creature entered and raped her. After the rape, the creature walked away out of sight and two soldiers walked back into the room, dressed her, and took her into another room for an examination. She recalled being strapped to a table, and someone shaved a small portion of her head behind her right ear. That person then wrote something on her head near her ear, and then she was given an intravenous shot and lost consciousness. Her next recollection was waking with her boyfriend on a nearby beach.

About ten years later, Michelle discovered an inflamed cyst behind one of her ears. She went to a doctor to have it removed. The object taken out was about the size of a bullet. The object, to our knowledge, has never been identified.

We're also pretty sure of one other thing. If there are people in our own government working with the aliens, there are also covert operations to learn as much as possible about the alien beings and their technology, if in fact we are forced to defend ourselves against them. A line said by Michael Corleone in *The Godfather Part II* applies here: "Keep your friends close and your enemies closer."

So, some abductees are reporting that there is a military(-like) presence during the abduction. Did our military learn interrogating and mind control from the aliens, or maybe our secret intelligence-gathering methods were given to the aliens? Any way you look at it, something sinister is going on.

Is our government working with aliens in abducting people for experiments? Is our government working on its own and blaming aliens? Or could it be that the aliens are abducting people and implanting thoughts in the abductees' heads, which the military allows so that we don't blame the aliens alone? Remember, aliens aren't the only ones good at head games. We will discuss this subject of governmental control in a later chapter of the book.

Control from Other People

Once you get past the idea of governmental control, you realize that some other people have some kind of control over you, such as parents, spouses, employers, and peers, as well as certain conditions of life. We have a lot more self-control over this factor, in that if we don't like the control we find ourselves involved with, we can make a change: leave home when old enough, quit a job and find a better one, find different friends or life partners. We also learn that we are not the only ones being controlled. We sometimes find that we are the controllers over someone else. We can lose that control the same way we can free ourselves; they can also.

It seems that we are easy to control. Not everybody is, but too many are letting others tell us how to live and what to do. There are many cults that have people so spellbound that they are even willing to take their own lives in the belief that it is for their betterment and that of their beliefs. A couple of these we mentioned earlier.

In November 1978, a group of 918 (some references say 909) members of the Peoples Temple in Jonestown, Guyana, took their own lives by drinking cyanide-laced Kool-Aid when instructed to by their cult leader, Jim Jones.

In October 1994, a group of forty-eight men, women, and children, all members of the Solar Temple cult, were found dead, all shot in the head in a supposed mass suicide in an underground Swiss chapel (www.Brainz.org).

In March 1997, a group of thirty-nine members of the Heaven's Gate cult took their own lives under instructions by cult leader Marshall Applewhite.

History is filled with other mass suicide stories of people who have been led to commit suicide because a cult leader has made them believe that it was the right thing for them to do.

Alien Control

The reason for this book is not so much to discuss all the control that we have or how our governments and fellow human beings control us, but to examine the control that we ourselves are under that we may not even know about or know how to get out from under. The world we live in is being visited. This is no longer a surprise, a myth, or a science fiction story. There are too many credible witnesses and experiencers to continue the lie that we are not being visited. One of the controls that our government has exercised deals with what we *believe*, what we *should* believe, and what we *should not* believe.

After all, the military has already proven how easily it can lie to us and manipulate and trick us into believing what they want us to. Look at the way they handled the Roswell UFO crash in 1947. A craft not of this world crashed. The military told the whole world that they had recovered a crashed UFO. It went all over the news—in the papers and on the radio. Calls were coming in from all over on the same day. The next day, the air force said that it was not a UFO but a weather balloon that had crashed. This was believed immediately. No one questioned it because of ignorance or fear of reprisal. Almost thirty years went by before an investigation into the matter took place, started by Stanton Friedman. Some years later, the air force again changed their story and the media accepted it—and so did most of the country.

The one thing that we can count on is that the UFO topic is linked to power and control. The information is controlled by the US government, either to protect us or them, but nonetheless it remains a guarded secret. Even if no proof ever comes from the government, we consider many of their knee-jerk answers almost an admission of guilt. Either they think most of the American people are ignorant to the point of believing anything they are told, or we really do have a few idiots in government.

In Roswell, truth seems to happen naturally and appeared to be an unconscious first response. The fact that they told the truth that a UFO had crashed outside Roswell and had been found by the military is what we consider an example of that unconscious first response. This was a local base response. They found it and wanted the world to know that the only nuclear bomber base in the world also had possession of a UFO! Front-page news and blowing their own horn, so to speak.

Then someone up the chain of command reported it or heard about it and put a cap on it to kill the story—thinking that something like that should be classified at least until they knew what they were dealing with and what type of technology could be gleaned from it. Okay, fine. We can understand their point, but look what happened next, and this still stuns us today. At that time (1947), we had built and perfected a working nuclear weapon. This was impressive technology for the day; then the order came to kill the crashed UFO story and come up with a plausible explanation. We don't know who came up with the weather balloon story, but we for the life of us cannot understand why so many people bought into it.

Just think about this for a second, and this is an old chain of thought: We certainly were not the first to come up with it. How can you tell us that personnel from a military air base, a nuclear air base no less, had people of high training and capabilities—and not to mention higher security classifications—who could not tell a crash craft of alien technology from beyond this world from a weather balloon? That's the dumbest hack job story we've ever heard. That makes no sense at all unless the people working there were truly idiots, and we don't believe that for a second either.

These people on base were around or flew planes every day. They knew aircraft. That would be like you driving a car to work every day and coming upon an automobile accident and misidentifying it as a boat crash! Even better, years later the air force came up with the story that the alien bodies involved in the UFO crash were actually test manikins thrown out of a plane. Can anyone reading this book say that if they found a smashed test dummy in pieces on the ground, they would accidentally identify it as an alien life form? The only test dummies here are the ones writing excuses for the US government to say that Roswell was totally explainable, and that it was not a UFO crash with dead alien bodies. These are both great examples of how information is controlled to control us.

09

IF UFOS AND THEIR OCCUPANTS *ARE* REALLY VISITING US, WHY?

IF THEY ARE VISITING US? AGAIN, MOST people have come to the conclusion that we are being visited on a regular basis. We have cave paintings showing humanoid beings coming out of the sky on flaming objects. Some are even drawn with what appear to be space helmets on, which have been on that cave wall for how many years? The stories of UFO sightings and abductions just keep coming.

The Mutual UFO Network (MUFON), the largest privately funded UFO research organization in the world, tells the *Huffington Post* that more people than ever are reporting unidentified flying objects, mostly in the United States and Canada. "Over the past year, we've been averaging 500 sighting reports a month, compared to about 300 three years ago [67 percent increase]," MUFON international director Clifford Clift said (*Huffington Post*, first posted August 26, 2011).

UFO Sighting Reports: According to multiple surveys over the last several decades and from different countries: 5–7% of people have seen a UFO, and 10–15% know someone who has seen a UFO. At least several hundred thousand (estimated) UFO sightings have been documented over the last 50 years, and the total number of UFO sightings is estimated to be in the millions. At least several thousand sightings are reported each year. Only

a small percentage of those who see a UFO report the sighting (www.
ufoevidence.org, July 15, 2012).

UFO Studies

The following are some major studies undertaken during the past fifty years
that reported on identification of UFOs:

- Project Blue Book Special Report No. 14 (referred to further below as
  BBSR) was a massive statistical study of 3,200 UFO cases between
  1952 and 1954 that the Battelle Memorial Institute did for the US Air
  Force. Of these, 22 percent remained and were classified as unidentified
  ("true UFOs"). Another 69 percent were deemed identified (IFOs). There
  was insufficient information to make a determination in the remaining
  9 percent.

- The official French government UFO investigation (GEPAN/SEPRA), run
  within the French space agency (CNES) between 1977 and 2004,
  scientifically investigated about 6,000 cases and found that 13 percent
  defied any rational explanation (UFOs), while 46 percent were deemed
  readily identifiable, and 41 percent lacked sufficient information for
  classification.

- The USAF-sponsored Condon Committee study reported that all
  117 cases studies were or could probably be explained. A 1971
  review of the results by the American Institute of Aeronautics and
  Astronautics concluded that 30 percent of the 117 cases remained
  unexplained.

- Of about 5,000 cases submitted to and studied by the civilian UFO
  organization NICAP, 16 percent were judged to be unknowns.

In contrast, much more conservative numbers for the percentage of
UFOs were arrived at individually by astronomer Allan Hendry, who was the
chief investigator for the Center for UFO Studies (CUFOS). CUFOS was
founded by astronomer Dr. J. Allen Hynek (who had been a consultant for
the air force's Project Blue Book) to provide a serious scientific investigation
into UFOs. Hendry spent fifteen months personally investigating 1,307 UFO
reports. In 1979, Hendry published his conclusions in *The UFO Handbook:
A Guide to Investigating, Evaluating, and Reporting UFO Sightings*. Hendry
admitted that he would like to find evidence for extraterrestrials but noted
that the clear majority of cases had prosaic explanations. He found 89
percent of reports definitely or probably identifiable, and only 9 percent
unidentified (Hendry 1979). "Hardcore" cases—well-documented events
that defied any conceivable conventional explanation—made up only 1.5
percent of the reports.

Let's take a quick look at a few numbers. The Mutual UFO Network states that 90 percent of all UFO sightings go unreported and that only 10 percent of the people are compelled to report a sighting.

MUFON averages 500 to 600 UFO sightings reported a month. If you accept that number as the 10 percent of the reported sightings, then we have the potential of a total of 5,000 to 6,000 UFO sightings a month! Even if you look at Allan Hendry's numbers above, which are very tough standards, and remove all the potentially explainable sightings each month, you are left with seventy-five "hardcore" UFO sightings that defy any explanation.

Let us put this into perspective for you. If you were informed by a reliable source that there were 500 to 600 reports a month of "Bigfoot" sightings, would you not almost automatically make the assumption that these creatures are real if that many reports were coming in? If only seventy-five of them were deemed "hardcore" reports, you would have people with guns and cages combing the forest looking for them.

Let's get even more ridiculous for a second. Let's say that we were getting a potential total of 5,000 to 6,000 sightings a month of leprechauns. Would you not start glancing for yourself to see if you could see one or start chasing for the ends of rainbows? Now we're not suggesting that Bigfoot or leprechauns are real or linked in any way to UFOs. We're just making fun with the numbers to prove a point.

The opening question, "Are we being visited?," is not even a question anymore. Look at the numbers yourself. Over 50 percent of the polled population believes that we are being visited. We might ask how many different types or kinds of beings are visiting us, but not *are* we being visited.

For too many years and to too many people, there has been the experience of alien abductions. Most alien abductions are done without any choice and without permission. After being abducted so many times, some people have come to accept it as a way of life in that there was no way to stop it, so they just bear it. Those who don't want it to happen have just as little choice about it. It will still happen, and very little has come to light to stop it. The reason for this is that we lack the knowledge of what is happening. Not enough scientific minds are focusing on the issue to provide answers. We are attempting to explain how it is happening and what we can do about it.

We do know that people have been reporting events of missing time, and during that missing time they are being used for reasons we do not truly understand. With almost sixty years of abduction accounts piling up, we know the basis. Humans are taken, fertile cells are removed by various methods, some people are implanted with objects, and some people are employed to help abduct others. Some abductees have been shown the result of the reproductive-cell harvesting: childlike hybrids that look like a cross between us and them, but very sickly looking with only wisp of hair. Then they are told that they are the parent of that childlike creature and are urged to hold and show affection toward that child. Touching of the child is very important to it surviving, and we will briefly mention this aspect later.

The abductee in this situation usually develops some kind of bonding with the child hybrid. They report a feeling of telepathic communication with the child, and the child recognizes them as one of its parents. The abductee, usually female, may even look forward to visiting with that child again and often does experience the feeling of loss at leaving behind the child aboard the craft.

Others who have been abducted are shown things that amaze them or open awareness to certain aspects of their lives or the lives of the people on the planet. Eventually, some of them seem to forget what it was that had happened to them, that they didn't want to happen. They forget that they had been kidnapped, repeatedly in most cases. They forget that they may have been raped or sexually abused. While we may be sounding dramatic, that is exactly what has happened in some cases: a rape, complete with broken bones and other injures. Even though they have had no control in the abduction of themselves or of their loved ones, on some level they may come to feel that it may be for the best.

When confronted with a situation of which they have no control, they may feel it is better to go with it; kind of like the old adage: when given lemons, make lemonade! Whether through bonding friendship or hypnotic mind transformation, they become emotionally attached to their abductors in some cases. This symptom bears a resemblance to what has been known as "Stockholm Syndrome," where the abductee looks forward to meeting with the abductors and wants to help them, primarily because they have no control in the matter anyway; why make it worse?

Stockholm Syndrome is a paradoxical psychological phenomenon in which hostages express positive feelings toward their captors, showing empathy toward them, sometimes to the point of defending them. Stockholm Syndrome was coined by the criminologist and psychiatrist Nils Bejerot in 1973, who assisted the police during the robbery of a bank in Stockholm, Sweden, to describe the management of hostages when some bank robbers kept the employees and customers of the bank hostage for five days before releasing them. When finally released, some of the hostages became emotionally attached to their captor. The FBI's Hostage Barricade Database System shows that roughly 27 percent of victims show evidence of Stockholm Syndrome (*Time*, April 29, 1974, by Jennifer Latsen).

In 1974, Patricia Hearst, the granddaughter of publishing magnate William Randolph Hearst, was kidnapped by the Symbionese Liberation Army. After a few months of captivity, she was seen aiding the group in bank robberies. When arrested and tried for robbery, her defense claimed Stockholm Syndrome for her reasoning.

During the 1950s and 1960s, people who felt this way and claimed that they could contact their space friends were called contactees. These people claimed to have started out as abductees and then decided that the aliens were friendly, and that they were looking out for our benefit and well-being. The contactees believed that we were doomed and that the aliens were here to save us from ourselves. Whether true or not, the abducted victim was now a co-conspirator with his or her kidnappers, something that bears its own psychological weight of guilt. Some even claimed to work with the aliens in abducting others so as to make it a better experience for the abductee, telling them it was "okay" and that it would be "over soon" and to "stay calm."

One fellow we ran into almost twenty years ago referred to himself as "the bus driver" because he was taught how to fly a smaller craft and go house to house, so to speak, with a group of Greys, picking up abductees for his captors. We recall him saying that he picked up people from a group of different states, and it took only minutes to fly from the Midwest to the Northeast to pick someone up. The Greys did the abducting with his help, as someone to calm the abductee.

Our initial response was to refer to him as "Benedict Arnold" instead of "the bus driver," but we quickly realized that he was not a bad guy, just one thrown into a tough situation, so he made the best of it. One could see that he was sincere about helping the other abductees.

MIND CONTROL AND ALIEN IMPLANTS

ET MAKES A "PHONE HOME" CALL:

Hello, Dad. I think my work is done down here. I've done my homework, and it's all complete. I've studied these people and am ready to come home. Please send the ship to pick me up. Where? I don't know if I can get there from here. I know! I will make the kid take me there on his bike. It won't be a problem. I can pretty much make them do whatever I want. Okay, see you soon.

Communication is a driving force, not only in this world, apparently, but in the universe. Without some kind of communication, we can't tell anyone what we want to do or what we want them to do. So, we talk, write, text, sign, use body language and facial expressions, or drop hints. That's how we communicate.

But how do aliens communicate among themselves and with us? Somehow, they must be able to tell each other things. There appears to be a hierarchy among them, and orders are obviously passed down the ranks. For instance, how does the head alien on the mother ship tell the Greys to go to someone's house and abduct them? Is their communication ship to ship, or direct and telepathically, and, if so, what is the range of direct telepathically sent communications? Is there a range or is it infinite; if you know, then how?

How do they know who is going, how do they know who is to render him or her helpless, and who is going to be the lead escort to the craft and when they come back? And who is going to have sex with him or her, and how do they know when to release the abductee? No one ever sees a clipboard or checklist with names on it.

Reports from abductees almost always indicate that aliens do not verbally talk. Their lips, which basically consist of just a slit opening, never move. The mouth does not seem to be used for ingestion of food *or* communications.

Paul Winchell would love to have one of them on his lap (well, maybe). For those who don't know of or remember him, Paul Winchell (December 21, 1922–June 24, 2005) was a great ventriloquist. Winchell's best-known ventriloquist dummies were Jerry Mahoney and Knucklehead Smiff. Winchell, who had medical training, was also an inventor, becoming the first person to build and patent a mechanical artificial heart, implantable in the chest cavity (US Patent #3097366). He has been honored with a star on the Hollywood Walk of Fame for his work in television, according to his bio on his website.

From all the studies and research on alien communication, it seems as though there are only two viable methods of aliens communicating with humans: telepathy or by implanting some device in the body capable of receiving a signal. After this book is published we'll probably be told there are others, but for now, this is what we know.

Abductees have said that the communication is usually heard inside their head, not by their ears. This sounds like telepathy. So, do they dabble in ESP? Can telepathy be heard by anyone or only chosen ones? Does one need to be "wired" differently to have telepathy or to pick it up as a receiver? Is that the choosing factor for abductees?

One abductee reported that every now and then he gets this thought in his head that he should go outside with his camera. He does, and within a few minutes a UFO flies by and he takes a picture of it. These instances have been documented in reports, and his photos have been analyzed, with no logical explanation for what they are. This has been reported by many abductees for other reasons.

Another example of alien communication is from Philip J. Imbrogno, a UFO researcher and author who wrote a paper titled "Extraterrestrial Contact: Are They Programming Our Minds?" In his paper he tells of a man who had some interesting UFO photos taken in Connecticut, within the Hudson River valley area that was made famous in a book written by Imbrogno along with J. Allen Hynek and Robert Pratt called *Night Siege: The Hudson Valley UFO Sightings*. The man called Imbrogno and told him that he had some good photos that he had taken of a UFO in his neighborhood, and that he had a few other neighbors with him at the time for verification. When Imbrogno looked at the photos, he was impressed, but when he heard how they were taken, he was even more impressed. The man said he gets a message in his head to go out, and a UFO will be there for him to photograph.

He would call his neighbors to come out to see it too, so he would have witnesses to verify his sighting and the taking of the pictures.

Also in this paper, Imbrogno wrote of a man who had an unusual kind of implant. He said this man had alien abduction experiences throughout most of his life, which started as a child. He began to think that the many contact experiences he had were so frequent that he started thinking it was normal. However, as he got older, the contacts stopped. Then when he got into his thirties, he had a particularly strange dream. He was sleeping in his bed one night when he was woken by a strange buzzing sound. When he looked around, his room was illuminated by a bluish light. He tried to move but could not. Then three small beings entered his room, wearing robes. As the three beings neared his bed, he noticed one of them carrying a bag. Each being surrounded him in the bed. One was on each side of him, and one was behind the bed near his head. Although he could not hear anything between them, he believed they were communicating among each other. He could still hear the buzzing sound. The being near his head seemed to be getting some instruments from the one with the bag. He thought they were doing some kind of surgical operation. It felt as if they had removed the top of his head and were poking around in his brain. He said he saw that one being's hand, the one nearest his head, was holding a multicolored crystal. He thought the crystal had been put into his brain. They then put the top of his head back on and ran out of the room. In the following weeks, he had a visit by some tall, blond beings who instructed him that he was to write down information regarding the true state of the universe. He was to write several manuscripts, which he did, finishing it all in three days; each of the volumes was 500 pages. He said that his head felt like it was on fire during this time. And he wrote it all in an unknown type of language with diagrams.

Earlier we mentioned that in the '50s and '60s, there were a rash of people claiming to be contactees. There are still some people who claim they can communicate with aliens almost any time they want to. These people claim that they can draw them down to where they can be seen or photographed, or even arrange (bus) trips to other planets. Maybe they can or maybe they just think they can. It hasn't been proven with many of them one way or the other.

Regardless, either way there is some kind of communication. Knowledge of another possible means of communication that has been reported by many abductees is from the discovery of implants found within parts of the body.

What Is an Implant?

Regarding this topic, an implant is anything that did not originate within the body and has been purposely implanted in the abductee's body to accomplish something. That might be as a communication device, or to monitor some biological function, such as when a woman is ovulating and ready for harvest. We don't mean to sound cold and clinical, but this appears to be how the aliens look at it, merely a job to be done with as little fuss and chitchat as possible.

The human body may have implants that we humans have put there as well. Some by accident, such war wounds and shrapnel, or it could be something as simple as a splinter in a finger, screws holding a broken ankle together, or a knee or hip replacement. It could be something as intricate as a tracking device or a receiving device.

How the body reacts to an object being implanted into it may differ with different individuals. Take for example something as simple as a splinter. A piece of wood or metal is not a normal object in the body, and to show its objection the body rejects it by swelling up, turning red, and causing pain. The splinter then must be removed to relieve the body of all discomfort. In part, the purpose of the swelling is to engorge the area with blood, macrophages, and lymphocytes to attack and try to break down the foreign body. Pressure builds that causes pain, but ideally the pressure either pushes out the foreign body the way it came in or ruptures the area to blow it out so it can heal.

For whatever reason a person needs to surgically have an implant, such as screws put into bone joints (usually because of a bone breakage), the body may not accept it, and as in the case of some knee replacement or hip replacement implants, the person may have to go through another surgery if the body rejects the screws or new joints. Sometimes it may have to be done many times. Not all surgical implants work successfully. GPS chips have been devised for implanting into human beings for tracking purposes by other human beings.

Animals are sometimes inserted with implants such as tracing devices. Some sharks have been inserted with tracking devices to follow migrating habits. Wild animals have also been implanted for the same reason. It is a normal and usually painless procedure. Sometimes the tracking device is nothing more than just a tag with contact information for someone to call back to the tracker.

When you buy a new automobile now, almost all of them have GPS devices put into them. Not just so you can find your way when lost, but also for security purposes, such as locating a stolen car or finding someone who has broken the law and escaped in a car with such a device. Unlike the human body or an animal's body, a GPS in an automobile cannot reject an implanted device. And for that matter, you may not even be aware that such a device is built into your vehicle. If it is, somebody always knows where you are, or at least where your car is. I'm sure it makes repo work a breeze these days: they no longer have to find the vehicle in question; they know within 10 feet where it is at all times. And so does anyone else who has the authority to procure that type of information. This is food for thought for you paranoids out there.

Although not all implants are accepted by the body it was put into, many are received by the body without issue. New materials have been developed that the body does not feel as a threat, so it leaves the implant alone and does not try to expel or reject it. Many times, there is little or no discomfort. Some people may forget or never even know there is one in them.

For the purpose of this book, we will be touching mostly on an unusual implant, one that may be used for tracking purposes or used to communicate with the subject. It may even be used to control an individual. As scary as it may seem, it may be possible that some people have been implanted with a device such as a chip that can do all these things. And it is done without the person's knowledge or permission. This is the implant that has been found in many alien abductees.

As we've mentioned, an alien abductee doesn't always know he or she has been abducted and usually doesn't know what has happened during the abduction. Some have reported having total recall of all events, and some may have had little recall, but mostly they have no recall unless it has been retrieved through various means such as dreams or flashbacks, and even then, through methods such as regressive hypnosis by a qualified and experienced hypnotherapist. Even in the recall, the abductee is not always aware that an implant had been inserted into them—although there have been some people who have a recollection of not being abducted but seeing something unusual fly up to them and touch them. Usually an alien implant is discovered by noticeable nosebleeds that occur for no apparent reason. Or an irritation in some part of the body that makes them uncomfortable, such as walking with an implant in a toe or part of the foot. Some abductees, having no recollection or knowledge of an implant, have had them found during routine doctor examinations, MRIs, PET scans, and X-rays for unrelated injuries. Others have found that an irritation causing them to rub an area often and hard enough has driven the object out. Some abductees have sneezed out an implanted device from their sinus cavity.

There is a report of a man—we'll call him Peter—who tells a story of when he was eight years old in 1955. He was walking in a wooded area of Troy, New York, with another young friend. They came across two small, unusual beings in the wooded area, and they started to approach them. As they got close, they noticed that there was a UFO on the ground nearby. Peter's friend immediately ran away in fear, but Peter didn't. Peter told me (Jim) that he couldn't resist when taken aboard the craft. "It was as if his will had been sapped," he said. He was able to recall going into the craft. He was given an implant and was told that he should never remove it. If he did, it would kill him, so he left the object where it was for many years, until, as an adult, one day he had rubbed the area enough so that the object had just fallen out. He contacted the MUFON state director at the time. The object was submitted to MIT for analysis. Since this was a very unusual object and not analyzed frequently, the lab didn't know what they were dealing with. They cut the object into two pieces and gave one half back to Peter to keep and analyzed the other half. Their finding was that the object was organic in nature, and nothing that could harm the body. The odd part about the object when they cut it in half was the observation of very tiny wire-like protrusions sticking out from the object.

A pioneer in the field of alien implants was Dr. Roger Leir. Dr. Leir was a podiatrist by trade and got into this field of study through the proddings by some members of the California branch of MUFON. Dr. Leir has over the years operated and removed many implants believed to be of alien origination. He has submitted the implants to various labs for analysis, not using only one. He has given many lectures and written a book about his work and the findings.

According to Dr. Roger Leir in his book *Alien Implants*, published by Whitley Strieber's Hidden Agenda series, tested implants have been analyzed and found to be fragments of metal encased in a membrane made of skin, which posed a problem because the implants have been found too deep in the body, deep enough that skin cannot grow.

The body is not capable of growing skin anywhere except on its surface. The body should reject the skin if it is grown internally. In the case of the implants recovered by Dr. Leir and sent to labs for analysis, the implants, covered in a membrane composed of surface tissue (skin), which should have been rejected by the body, had managed to survive in the body for years.

Sample implants had been sent to labs at New Mexico Tech by NIDS, the National Institute of Discovery Science. The lab was not told what the sample was or where it came from. Their findings were that the metallic fragments were probably meteoric.

Another instance of an implant with similar characteristics is from a man named John Smith (presumably not his real name). Mr. Smith has had a history of alien abductions. One night, Mr. Smith had an encounter with two (unusually large) raccoons. He fed the animals for a while and then watched them. Later that evening he went to bed and then woke up the next morning with a very painful toe and soreness on the side of his head. Upon examination of the toe, it was discovered that there were two small puncture marks on the side of the toe and a small scratch on the other side. The severity of the soreness in his toe increased over the next four days. Eventually, Mr. Smith went to see Dr. Leir for an examination of the toe. Dr. Leir obtained X-rays of the toe. Upon examining the X-rays, they discovered a very small object similar to a bent wire embedded in the toe, and the wire-like object had the same density as a human bone. A CAT scan was done on the toe, and it revealed that there was a foreign object there.

Dr. Leir performed a Gauss meter and radio frequency test on the object. These tests indicated that the object was emitting radio waves in the gigahertz, megahertz, and extremely low frequency (ELF) bands. The object also generated a magnetic field of more than 10 milliGauss (mG).

The object was removed, and in the process it broke into twelve tiny fragments. The fragments turned black and then red when put into a blood serum and into a refrigerator. Within twelve hours of removal from the toe, the pieces of the object had lined up back into the original shape it had been.

Is it possible for the implant to be a means of controlling the abductee? Is it possible that the implant is actually a foreign body inserted into humans by aliens? As mentioned earlier in this chapter, we use implants on animals to track them and learn their habits. Wouldn't it be great if we could put an implant in an animal and control them? Imagine having a dog with such a control. No more leashes needed, and you can get them to come home with a quiet signal. Wildlife could be tamed. A shark in the water could be controlled to swim away from people in the water. The list of imaginative possibilities could go on and on.

According to Steven Colbern, a chemist and materials scientist with A & S Research who did some of the analysis work for Dr. Leir:

The John Smith implant was a metallic object, recovered from Mr. Smith's left, second toe, was apparently made of meteoric iron, and contained inclusions of carbon nanotubes (CNTs). The CNTs most likely functioned as nanoelectronics and electrical wiring. The object was giving off radio signals before removal, had a 10 milliGauss magnetic field, and was obviously a sophisticated nanotechnological device.

The device had the typical gray, electrically conductive, membrane around it, which has been seen in most of the implants removed from Dr. Leir's patients. This membrane was connected to the nervous system by proprioceptor receptor nerves, as has also been the case in many other implant cases. Large CNT bundles coming out of the metallic portion of the object appeared to be the main electrical connections to the device.

The device produced no immune response to its presence in Mr. Smith's body, as is the case with all other alien implants removed and studied thus far. This is completely unprecedented, and has only been seen in the case of these objects; all other known materials produce a measurable immune response to their presence in the human body.

Under hypnosis, Mr. Smith remembered the typically reported small, Grey-skinned, aliens as the ones who had implanted the device in his toe. Mr. Smith had the impression that the device functioned mainly as a physiological monitor, but also felt a distinct difference in his thought patterns and subjective feelings after its removal.

What would it take to create such an implant? Microchips for tracking are already in implementation, but can we create something to control? Scientists have grown rat brain neurons on the surface of a silicon chip. Case in point here: How about a robot being controlled by rat brains? Kevin Warwick, a researcher in cybernetics at the University of Reading, has been working on creating neural networks that can control machines. He and his team have taken the brain cells from rats, cultured them, and used them as the guidance control circuit for simple wheeled robots. Electrical impulses from the robots enter the batch of neurons, and responses from the cells are turned into commands for the device. The cells can form new connections, making the system a true learning machine (http://singularityhub.com).

So, now we have communication between rat brain neurons and mechanical devices. We have implants that look like bits of meteoric material but have smaller, unique parts hidden from normal microscopes. It is not unlike the discovery of bacteria. Antony Leeuwenhoek was the first person to see bacteria. He revolutionized biological science by exposing microscopic life to the world, and his findings of what he called "animalcules" were confirmed by the Royal Society of London in 1676 (www.experiment-resources.com). We did not really know it existed until we developed a microscopic way to observe it. By the way, Leeuwenhoek created over 400 different types of microscopes during his career.

We believe that the alien implants function largely on the nanoscale and therefore carry on the prescribed business right under our noses, because most implants never end up under an electron scanning microscope or have someone who can recognize the molecular structure of the carbon nanotubes or other atomic-sized level of nanomachines. The US is currently spending billions of research dollars on nanotechnology, which is the manipulation of matter on a molecular and atomic scale. Generally, nanotechnology works with materials, devices, and other structures sized from 1 to 100 nanometers; a nanometer is one billionth of a meter. Quantum mechanical effects are important at this quantum-realm scale (we will get into that in a later chapter).

An interesting thought: We have heard of abductees sneezing out a pellet or finding some small implant that could be removed; they put it in a glass jar, and in a matter of hours it just disappears! If the implants are literally pieced together on an atomic scale and are a group of nanomachines, could they also detect when they are removed from the abductee's body and literally take themselves apart, effectively seeming to disappear? If a group of nanomachines, built out of a hundred or so atoms apiece, could scatter and spread out, could they not possibly hide on the surface of the glass jar or, if mobile, escape somehow?

We imagine we would require some kind of trigger mechanism that is hooked up to the brain in order for the communication to be understood, and then it will require some kind of force to make the subject do as instructed. We have an autonomic nervous system that functions automatically and runs such things as our heartbeat and digestion. You don't need to consciously think to make your heart beat or to digest food. If an implant could tap into the autonomic system, it might circumvent the conscious brain.

Hypnotism definitely won't do it, because we still have that internal control that we can't really be hypnotized into doing something that we do not want to do. But if someone who is hypnotized into thinking that what he or she is instructed to do is what they *believe* they want to do, then all bets are off. This is covered more in the section on hypnosis.

So, let's say we can put an implant into someone. And let's say that it is not rejected by the body because we were able to coat the implant with a bone- or skin-like membrane. Now this object must also be capable of receiving some kind of radio transmission. How would we be able to get the transmission signal to the brain to tell it what to do? Some of the recovered implants have been found in the head, such as in the nasal cavity, in or near the ear, and around the neck. It still must be connected to a nerve. Dr. Eddie Bullard, a UFO researcher and author of *UFOs and Abductions*, tells of one case where the abductee recalled her eye being pulled from the socket, and an implant was placed deep into her brain.

Can an implant be inserted directly into the brain and not be detected? And if so, why are so many implants found in other parts of the body? Could some be used just for tracking while others are used for tracking and control? If possible, why would they use different kinds when one type could fit all purposes?

What would an implant be like and how could it function in the body?

It must be small enough to be able to be inserted into an area of the body that won't be noticed—usually deep into the body so it won't easily come out. It must contain a power source, such as a battery, but still be very, very small. The battery will also have to have a source for recharging.

Why can't abductees remember that they were abducted?

How does memory work? And what causes us to forget, and do we forget abductions on our own or are we made to forget? How does the brain work?

In the June 2011 issue of the *MUFON UFO Journal* (volume 518), an article by journal editor Janice Currie relates the event of two young boys who were camping out in a field behind one of their homes in 1964. Shortly after midnight, one of the boys noticed a disk-shaped object floating over some nearby trees, heading toward the house. Suddenly, a very bright light came on, and one of the boys saw a face up close staring into his eyes. He thought it was his friend looking at him. The next thing he remembered, he was standing out in another part of the yard, looking at the light in the sky leaving. Neither of the two boys talked about it because they could not remember it for twenty years, and then both boys, now adults, remembered the event almost at the same time, even though they were living hundreds of miles away.

11

MEMORY

Human and Computer

Most of us are familiar with only two types of memory: the memory stored in our brain and the memory used for storage in a computer. As to how these types of memory work, most of us either don't know or don't care, as long as they continue to work.

Memory is stored on a chip in a computer, and biological memory, being totally different, cannot really be compared to a computer—although it is, continually so. Computers do mainly one thing at a time and work in series. To prove this, the next time your computer slows down while loading a program, push the enter key about a hundred times and see how much faster it does not work. That of course has changed in the past few years with dual and quad processors.

Brains do trillions of things all at the same time and work in parallel. You can chew gum and have your heart keep beating and your pancreas keep secreting all at the same time, but you don't have to consciously think about your heart and pancreas to make them work. One sidenote here: Did you ever notice that, most of the time, the only time you bite your tongue is when you are concentrating on where your tongue is while chewing? How long have you been chewing food? The muscle memory of your tongue and brain are better at operating your tongue than you are. Good thing your tongue isn't controlled by a joy stick!

Humans continuing to compare human memory functions to computer memory is like comparing an aardvark to a toaster. One is alive, and one is not; much past that, you can't toast an aardvark, and an aardvark won't eat toast. Well, I suppose you could toast an aardvark, but why would you want to? Moving along . . .

Computers crash and files are lost, and brains get damaged and memories get lost. A computer's memory chip consists of millions of miniature transistors and capacitors acting as on or off switches. The capacitor holds the bit of information—a 0 or a 1 (binary code), and the transistor acts as a switch that lets the control circuitry on the memory chip read the capacitor. A capacitor that stores an electron is a one (1), and one that is empty is a zero (0).

Computer memory rarely goes bad, but when it does, it's usually a catastrophic failure and a total loss. Brains may lose memories, but not all memories like a computer does. In the case of the computer, the memory is gone (i.e., does not exist); in the case of the brain, unless damaged by trauma or pathology, the memory is usually there but is misfiled or temporarily lost. How many of you have said to yourself, "I know that I know the answer; I just can't remember it," or have said, "I know that I know this, or at least I did know it," and continue to probe the deeper recesses of your mind for a clue to jiggle the answer loose. We never know that some lost or misfiled memories are even gone until we need the information or something triggers the process that says, "Hey, I used to know that."

Brains store memory in many ways and areas. A memory is information that may come in the form of images, such as with visual memory. It may be auditory, and we remember certain sounds or voices. It could be an odor or scent that triggers memory. There is even muscle memory that is stored in the muscles that do many repetitive motions, such as those practiced in many types of physical sports such as martial arts.

How Much Memory Does the Human Brain Have the Capacity to Hold?

As we said, one should not compare brains to computers, but here we go again. Do some people forget their abduction experience because they just run out of storage space? Is such a thing even possible? In the May 2010 issue of *Scientific American*, Paul Reber, professor of psychology at Northwestern University, was asked, "What is the memory capacity of the human brain?" Reber stated:

The human brain consists of about one billion neurons. Each neuron forms about 1,000 connections to other neurons, amounting to more than a trillion connections. If each neuron could only help store a single memory, running out of space would be a problem. You might have only a few gigabytes of storage space, similar to the space in an iPod or a USB flash drive. Yet neurons combine so that each one helps with many memories at a time, exponentially increasing the brain's memory storage capacity to something closer to around 2.5 petabytes (or a million gigabytes). For comparison, if your brain worked like a digital video recorder in a television, 2.5 petabytes would be enough to hold three million hours of TV shows. You would have to leave the TV running continuously for more than 300 years to use up all that storage.

This explains a lot, such as why we can remember the catchy jingle of a 3:00 a.m. infomercial while sound asleep in front of the TV. Apparently, we left the recorder in our heads on as well. Suffice it to say that, except in the case of some types of disease or brain injury, none of us have to worry about running out of space anytime soon. We must worry about where we put it.

How Is Memory Stored?

In a computer, memory is referred to as RAM or random-access memory. Our personal memories can be pretty random as well, especially when we really need to know something, and we try to force our brain into retrieving it. As we stated just previously, we know it's in there; we just must find it.

At this point we will dispense with talking computer memory, since it has nothing to do with the memory we are talking about. So enough of that . . . back to brains.

The brain obtains the input for the memory it stores through our five basic senses—sight, touch, hearing, taste, and smell. Many would argue, especially abductees, that there is really a sixth sense that some are connected into; in fact, maybe all of us are connected into it—just that some either ignore the input or lack the access code to connect, so to speak. We believe that to be true as well, and will discuss it later on.

Each thing that we experience through these senses is stored in the brain, so we are able to recognize the input from our senses and learn about them when we come across them again. In other words, if we were to, for example, go into a bakery, smell and see a delicious cake on a stove, go over to it to take a piece, burn our hand on the hot stove, hear the baker yell at us for touching the stove, then eat some of the cake, whenever we think about that experience or whenever we go into a bakery, we will most likely reexperience the whole episode again because we will remember it. The memory is being searched, reconstructed, and reinforced.

The memories we store are usually only two types, although there are three types of brain memory—immediate, short term, and long term. Immediate memory isn't used for storage as it is a staging area to determine what to do with the information. It's a place where we sort through input data very quickly to determine if it has any significance to us. Immediate memory holds data for two seconds or less, then either sends it on to short-term or working memory or dumps it. Talk about a short memory!

Short-term memory is information from input that is learned and used, often referred to as working memory, and then forgotten when no longer needed; for example, the request to "stop at the store and pick up some bread." Often this short-term memory is forgotten before we get to the bread aisle, and we buy something else that seems like a good idea at the time. My wife, on the other hand, is not impressed. She may now have Doritos, but still no bread.

Short-term memory appears to function in the hippocampus, which is a staging area for clusters of data that are going to be selected to be sent to long-term memory or just forgotten when the working function of the memory is done. Decision theorist Herbert Simon says that it takes about eight seconds of attention to add one new chunk to short-term memory. Can't remember someone's name? Concentrating on it for more than eight seconds greatly improves your chances.

Long-term memory is when something learned is needed to be recalled again sometime later. An example of short-term memory would be when you might see a car drive by and you notice the color of the car. When the car is gone, you will forget the color of the car because you do not need to remember it because it is not important enough. An example of long-term memory would be when you meet someone you will be working with, and you learn that person's name. When you meet that person again (if you are like me), you will have no idea what their name is anyway and will have to ask. Remember, name + eight seconds of concentration = memory of that person's name.

Long-term memory seems to be in the cerebral cortex, which is a sheet of neural tissue that is outermost to the cerebrum of the mammalian brain. It covers the cerebrum and cerebellum and is divided into left and right hemispheres. Memory appears to be nonlocal in the cerebral cortex or at least highly redundant. In animal studies, 20 percent of portions of the cerebral cortex were removed from various areas of the cortex. At 20 percent removal, memory did not seem to be affected. In other words, the information or memory was stored in multiple areas, so removing 20 percent from various areas did not result in memory loss. It was not until larger percentages of cortex were removed that memory was affected (Pierce J. Howard, PhD, *The Owner's Manual for the Brain: Everyday Applications from Mind-Brain Research*, 3rd ed., 2006).

When we learn something or see something, it is received into the hippocampus portion of our brain. This is a portion of the brain that was thought to be the memory storage area. However, it has been learned that the hippocampus converts short-term memories into long-term memories. The memories are then transferred and stored in other portions of the brain (http://101.com: Stress, Depression, and Memory Loss).

Henry Holcomb, a memory researcher at Johns Hopkins University's Department of Radiology, has determined that memory for a new motor skill takes up to five to six hours to move from the temporary storage in the front of the brain to permanent storage in the back of the brain. And that attempting to learn a new skill set before this five-or-six-hour period is up will cause problems for prior learning (Pierce J. Howard, PhD, *The Owner's Manual for the Brain: Everyday Applications from Mind-Brain Research*, 3rd ed., 2006).

According to James McGaugh, a psychobiologist at the University of California, Irvine, a key to the formation of long-term memories is the levels of neural transmitters such as epinephrine, also known as adrenaline, and norepinephrine. Norepinephrine tells the brain to hang on to that memory. Inhibit norepinephrine and long-term memory suffers. Epinephrine and norepinephrine are released by the adrenal medulla in the adrenal glands when the body is subjected to emotional or physical stresses.

Two physical causes of memory loss are stress and depression. When one becomes stressed, evidence indicates that stress hormones released from the adrenal glands are critically involved in memory. When we become stressed or anxious, our bodies also release epinephrine (adrenaline) into the bloodstream, which in turn causes the body to release glucocorticoids, also known as cortisol. You may have heard cortisol referred to as the stress hormone. The two compounds are an essential part of your fight-or-flight response but are very different from one another. One of the major differences is that cortisol remains in your body much longer than adrenaline does. Cortisol disrupts the normal function of neurotransmitters. The neurotransmitters, as mentioned above, are the chemicals used by brain cells to carry information (to be remembered), and if they are disrupted by cortisol, your brain has a difficult time sorting things out. Cortisol will cause damage to the cells of the hippocampus, affecting memory function. The more prolonged the stress, the more damage there is.

According to Joe Dispenza, the author of the book *Evolve Your Brain: The Science of Changing Your Mind* (2007), acute stress is unavoidable, but the longer a depression or stress occurs, the more permanent damage and shrinking of the hippocampus happens (http://101.com: Stress, Depression, and Memory Loss).

Another section of the brain that encodes memory is the amygdala, which is believed to be involved in the encoding and retrieval of emotionally charged memories. Much of the evidence for this has come from research on a phenomenon known as flashbulb memories. These are instances in which memories of powerful emotional events are more highly detailed and enduring than regular memories (e.g., the shuttle *Challenger* explosion, the 9/11 towers burning). Just the thought of something like this promotes more hormones being secreted to ingrain the memory even more.

Bottom line in all of this is that the hormones produced by the body in response to stress and fight-or-flight mode can both make our memory of a traumatic nature more ingrained, so it is always clear, and also muddle up the works and make things fuzzy. The chemical neural transmitters are released at the same time and in some ways counteract each other in an attempt at keeping homeostasis.

Homeostasis is the maintenance of metabolic equilibrium within us by a tendency to compensate for disruptive changes—essentially a series of countermeasures built into our brains and bodies to compensate for overexcitation, to keep us on an even keel or to be more balanced.

Storage of Memories by the Body and Manipulation by Other Forces

Earlier we mentioned that there were two basic types of memory used for storage, short term and long term, with immediate memory just used as a superfast staging area. We now know it takes five to six hours for temporary memory storage from the front of the brain to transition to permanent storage in the back of the brain. We know that memory is stored in multiple places in the brain and has redundant copies or, rather, possesses the ability to reconstitute a memory from multiple locations in the cerebral cortex. We know that the human brain has basically unlimited storage capacity, more than enough for the amount of experiences in our biological lifetime, and we know it is nothing like a computer . . . but will we remember these facts?

So, at this point, are the memories carved in stone, or just a bunch of gray mush? We have now determined that certain traumatic memories that we would rather forget are here forever, and the things we would like to remember forever seem to be fleeting. Memories that we think about often are easier to construct or reconstitute and stay fresher in our mind. Memories that you have not tried to bring forward from the backroom storage area in years are harder to reconstitute and seem less clear and detailed. Or just gone all together; but are they really gone?

Some experts say that you never really forget anything. Neurobiologist Jeffrey Johnson of the University of California, Irvine, said: "Even though your brain still holds this information, you might not always have access to it." Johnson coauthored a study published in *Neuron* magazine, a biweekly, peer-reviewed scientific journal of neuroscience published by Cell Press. "It wasn't quite clear what happens to them," said Johnson of lost details. "But even when people claim that there are no details attached to their memories, we could still pick some of those details out."

Johnson's team put sixteen college students inside an fMRI machine (one at a time, of course), which measures real-time blood flow in the brain. Students were shown a list of words, then asked to say each word backward, think of how it could be used, and imagine how an artist would draw it. The learning and memory process within the brain was mapped and recorded via increased blood flow in the fMRI.

Twenty minutes later, the researchers showed them the list again and asked the students to remember what they could of each word. Recalling the memories triggered the original learning patterns of blood flow in the fMRI, a process known as reinstatement; the stronger the memory, the stronger the signal. But at the weak end of the gradient in the study, where the students' conscious recall had faded to zero, the signal was still there; not consciously recalled, but not gone either! While the students could not recall anything about the word, the area of the brain that had learned the original word lit up with blood flow, suggesting that while not making it to the conscious mind for whatever reason, the information of that memory was being accessed. "We can only speculate that this is the case," said Johnson, who plans to run brain-imaging studies of memory degradation over days and weeks.

We personally would like to see a larger study group done to help factor out things that might affect the performance of the test, such as nutrition, amount of sleep, performance anxiety, and the fact that the students could become mentally taxed and tired and take short cuts, just wanting the test to be over, thus skewing the results. After all, thinking is hard work; it requires vast amounts of blood flow to the brain and caloric consumption. The brain is the only organ in the human body to use a whole 20 percent of the blood supply by itself.

If these results are accurate, then memory may truly persist. The question then is going to be how long can memories last, without reinstatement, and yet be fully intact but be only partially recoverable or not at all. And why would a study like this, which entailed no trauma to affect memory and involved students who wished to participate and presumably had healthy brains to begin with, have a memory spectrum ranging toward zero for some at the low end?

As for whether those memories could be intentionally guided to the surface, Johnson says that "At this stage, we're just happy to be able to find evidence of reinstatement at a weak level. That would be something down the line."

Memory-Editing Drugs: The Good, the Bad, and the Ugly

The development of drugs that control chemicals in the brain that are used to form memories has sparked scientific and philosophical speculation. Scientists recently used an experimental drug in animal testing that when delivered to the brain could block the activity of a substance that the brain needs to retain information in such areas as emotional associations, spatial knowledge, or motor skills, but other memory-blunting drugs are being tried in soldiers with post-traumatic stress disorder. We are one step away from having memories pharmaceutically erased, just as moods are chemically changed now. Of course, some of the mood-changing drugs may make you suicidal, but other than that, they are fine.

Now, we don't know where you weigh in on the mood-altering drugs, and perhaps you are one of the many whom they work fine for. The others whom it did not work well for are not reading this book because they may have "offed" themselves and are now dead. If this statement makes you uneasy, wait until the use of memory drugs starts! It used to be alcohol that made you forget, but that is what helped create alcoholics, because the effect of memory loss was only temporary. Memory-erasing drugs have the potential for some beneficial uses, such as in forgetting a horrifying trauma, but look at the potential to lose control of your memory.

We can be control freaks at times, and the thought of not being in control of our own memories makes us more than a bit nervous. This book is about various forms of control and the alien abduction phenomenon. The whole premise is based on anecdotal evidence derived from people's memories, and how it relates to our biology and the sciences necessary to make these events happen.

The aliens have the ability to mess with recall, and now we are actively working on man-made drugs to "edit" memory. The potential for abuse is enormous, and not just on a personal scale. We could see the darker side of some government factions being very interested in not having to control or intimidate a witness anymore. Just slip them a drug and the problem is gone. We might also mention that with the enormous list of drugs with crazy-bad side effects these days, who knows what will come as side effects from mind-erasing drugs (isn't mind erasing bad enough?).

Some say this represents an opportunity to eliminate the crippling psychic effects of trauma from one's past. Others might see a possibly harmful chemical intrusion into a system within our brain that essentially makes us who we are.

Our fears and memories exist for a reason: Fears remind us to be careful about things. If we are given a drug to forget our fears, for example, we might be drowning, play in traffic, or think that jumping out of a perfectly good airplane is a good idea. (Side note: Heights personally scare us; jumping out of a plane is not happening by choice. In fact, it would likely take at least six people to push either of us out of the plane door.)

Painful memories certainly are, well, . . . painful, but what good would it do to get rid of those memories, especially if they are recurring like an abductee's. As we have stated before, the worst thing about an abductee not being able to remember is the fact that they are terrified, as if the abduction is a new experience every single time they are taken. No recognition of "Oh no, it's happening again," just the initial shock, over and over and over. If that doesn't sound like some type of mental torture, we don't know what does. So yes, memory of even the bad things is crucial to us being who we are, and even improves our chances at survival. As Shakespeare wrote in *Hamlet:* "for there is nothing either good or bad, but thinking makes it so."

Oxford University neuroethicist Anders Sandberg talks about the future of memory-editing drugs. In some ways, Sandberg says:

Our memories are already being altered. We just don't realize it. A lot of discussion is based on the false premise that they'll work as well as well-studied, well-understood drugs like aspirin that have side effects that can be annoying or even dangerous. I think the same thing will go for memory editing. Current research seems to suggest that it can be specific, but there will be side effects. It may not even be that you forget other memories. Small, false memories could be created. And we're probably not going to be able to predict that before we actually try them. The problem is that it's the falsehoods that really mess you up. If you don't know something, you can look it up, remedy your lack of information. But if you believe something falsely, that might make you act much more erroneously.

Sandberg went on to say that we can't trust our memories, which we think is a bit of an overstatement. In our own memories, we might have been faster, more athletic, or better looking back then than is actual fact (we know we were). But on the other hand, out of a hundred million drivers on the road yesterday, who woke up this morning and could not remember how to drive? Or work on their computer or, for that matter, the words to a song from 1962.

Okay, that excludes a few of you, but you get the point. On the other hand, our memories are the basis for most of our decisions. Now, I (Bob) have a slightly bad memory. I do not always trust the smaller details of what I remember. That is why I have a huge resource library in my home. Let's say for the sake of argument that I was taught how to disarm a bomb thirty years ago and had never done it, but today was the day . . . oh boy, is it reference time. Is it the blue wire or the yellow wire? It was yellow, right? Maybe all this is good, because it forces us to recognize that the nature of our memory is not perfect. It is not carved in stone, but gray mush.

We take it as a given that we can trust our memory, and we should most of the time, but sometimes memories are problematic, as will we see in the next section, on the seven sins.

The Seven Sins and Other Sevens

Have you ever noticed how many things are associated with the number seven? The seven deadly sins, the Seven Wonders of the World, the seven habits of highly effective people, etc. I (Bob) can sit at my desk and gaze at my personal library and see at least six titles that consist of the seven of "something." (I believe that I have a seventh title, but I do not remember where I put it.)

In 1956, cognitive psychologist George A. Miller of Princeton University's Department of Psychology discovered the cognitive limitation of memory span. Memory span refers to the longest list of items (e.g., digits, letters, and words) that a person can repeat back immediately after presentation in correct order on 50 percent of trials. The human brain seems to easily remember up to seven digits in a row most of the time. Barring area code, how many digits in your phone number? Coincidence? If your phone number was a twenty-digit number, would you have any hope of remembering it when someone asks for your number?

We know that may make our immediate memory sound somewhat pathetic, being able to remember only seven things in a row, but remember, humans have the largest brain per body mass of any creature on this planet. A computer can remember a twenty-digit number with no problem but would not be able to understand the concept of the story of "Little Red Riding Hood." We can remember only seven digits in a row, reliably, but understand the concept and build the computer that remembers the twenty digits. Score another one for the gray mush.

Speaking of brain size: The alien creatures, the Greys, that so many people report, have thin, almost pipe-cleaner bodies with huge, bulbous heads. Most people jump right to the conclusion that they have big brains and must be cognitively superior. Other than their ability to communicate nonverbally through what we assume to be an attribute of their mental ability, we do not know if they are truly superior or just from a different neighborhood! Honeybees communicate nonverbally too. Who is smarter, you or the bee?

Maybe the aliens' organs for normal body functions are located in their head as well. Maybe they are of a hive mentality and have very small brains to make room for other organs that will not fit into their sticklike bodies. Food for thought. (The military probably knows for sure, since we suspect that they have dissected one or two of them over the years, starting with the Roswell crash of 1947.)

Since so much of the alien abduction phenomenon comes either from conscious or subconscious memories for information about the subject, we should investigate the mechanisms that both plague and enhance human memory. The more we understand about memory, the more we can glean from the information supplied by it. Not all memories are correct or even real, while others are very correct and extremely real. The slow but constant drip of abductees coming forward over the last fifty years has been easy for scientists to overlook, especially when some of them look at memory as so fallible. But one can only blame memory or say the phenomenon is "all in their head" for just so long before the drip of the last fifty years fills the bucket to the brim. If a million people all woke on the same day with memories of an abduction, would it be snubbed by science, denied by government officials, and ridiculed by those who did not experience it? Probably.

In 2001, Daniel L. Schacter wrote the book *The Seven Sins of Memory: How the Mind Forgets and Remembers*. He is the former chair of the Department of Psychology at Harvard University. His research has focused on psychological and biological aspects of human memory and amnesia, with a particular emphasis on the distinction between conscious and nonconscious forms of memory and, more recently, on brain mechanisms of memory distortion.

Professor Schacter has remarkable insight into the memory process, and we would like to show how his seven sins of memory relate to the abduction experience. The first three of the seven, so called "transgressions," are described as omissions, since they result in a failure to recall a fact, event, or idea. These are transience, absentmindedness, and blocking:

Transience refers to the general deterioration of specific memories over a lengthy amount of time. Much more can be remembered of recent events than past ones. This is especially true with autobiographical memory; these are memories from our past that, every time they are recalled, are re-encoded within the hippocampus, altering each memory a little each time you recall it because it is essentially being reconstituted or constructed within the neural pathways.

1. Transience

Transience might be a factor with alien abduction—if you had only been abducted once in your life and it was, say, fifty years ago. Unless you were an accidental abductee, truly in the wrong place at the wrong time (like the young boy who stayed over at a friend's house the same night the whole family was abducted, including him), most abductees are taken repeatedly over their useful lifetime. We say "useful" because it can and does stop for some when they are no longer of any use to the aliens (e.g., no longer fertile, not healthy, have become problematic). Thus, if the original memory is relived by concurring abduction events, transience is unlikely to any extent due to the memory not being re-encoded, but reinforced with fresh detail each time it occurs.

2. Absentmindedness

This one is my (Bob) personal favorite and one that I know intimately well. This form of memory breakdown involves problems at the point where attention and memory interface. I have a slight case of ADD myself, and it wreaks havoc with me when sleep or diet is off. It creates errors by inattention, and it creates common errors such as "Where are my glasses?" (usually shoved up on top of my head). What was I to pick up at the store? Or forgetting almost anything because at that moment it was deemed trivial, and at the time of encoding, insufficient attention was paid, and the memory that would be needed for recall later did not get properly stored.

We do not feel that absentmindedness is a factor with abductees' memories, if for no other reason than people tend to be on high alert during an event where something is strange or scary. Adrenaline is pumped into your system, the heartbeat increases, your respiration jumps, and fight-or-flight mode is prepped in extreme cases. When was the last time you fell asleep or did not remember how the scary movie ended because you were not paying attention while watching it?

Now, I am talking normal internal functions within your gray mush here. I am pretty sure that if I am watching a UFO land in my side yard while I am focusing on making my poached eggs, I will be distracted by the UFO.

However, externally, if the UFO is affecting my brain in some way to make my attention less focused on it than the poached eggs, we (or I) could potentially have a problem. We see abductees experience an event and then just go back to sleep or forget to take a picture of the craft when a camera is in the car, or just forget to talk about it for sometimes years after the event with people who shared the event.

This is not absentmindedness; this is manipulation of the brain's systems by an external force.

3. Blocking

Blocking refers to trying to recall information that has not faded out of memory but is temporarily inaccessible at that time. It may be forgetting a name of an associate (most common) whom you have not seen in a while, or a word for a sentence you started that refuses to "pop into your head"—and all are things that you know, you know! The connection is just not being made.

This is experiencing a block. An actor could block on their lines they had to orate on stage. You could blank on the name of a state or of the name of someone's spouse you are required to introduce—stuff that you know is in there but for some reason refuses to come to light, no matter how hard you try to make your brain power through it. It's going to take its sweet time to process. Or, at least you are hoping impatiently that it does.

There are even rare cases of blocking on personal information, such as with amnesia in which people are unable to recall large aspects of their past and even their own identity (Kihlstrom and Schacter 2000; Klein et al. 2002).

This type of "block" is more of the "it's right on the tip of my tongue" type of stuff that just refuses to "connect." This is not like the Freudian type of repressed memories that we think everybody tends to jump to in this case. We are not talking repression here, which is deliberate. This type of blocking is more incidental. This type of blocking is either simple information that is not recalled very often or information that does not have much of a database within memory to form clues to find it and be brought forward.

In the 1990s, an ugly debate developed over the accuracy of traumatic memories that had reportedly been forgotten for decades in some cases, which had been "recovered" in psychotherapy or because of some triggering event. One side argued that the memories were virtually accurate, and the other side held to the possibility that they were virtually false. Although the debate still rages, studies suggest that both are possible and indeed likely.

While some trauma can result in inhibited thought retrieval due to someone not wanting to remember, most studies show that trauma tends to make memories more vivid and ingrained making them just the opposite, harder to forget. Traumatic experiences may become blocked by "directed forgetting." This term refers to forgetting that is initiated by a conscious goal to forget (Baddeley et al. 2009) or intentional forgetting (repression), which is important at the individual level: suppressing an unpleasant memory of a trauma or a loss that is particularly painful (Freud 1946, originally published 1936).

Experiments also show when some people are given the suggestion to forget, their memories do seem to suffer. The classic hypnotist movie line of "you will remember nothing" does bear some weight if the hypnosis is done to a highly suggestible subject. The alien beings tell abductees that they will not remember until sometime in the future. This is while the abductee is often in some type of controlled, altered state—not unlike a hypnotist, except that we believe the level of control on the alien being's part is much more internal and direct.

4. Misattribution

Misattributing is the source of memories. People regularly say they read something in the newspaper, when actually a friend told them, or they saw it on the television newscast. In one study, participants with "normal" memories regularly made the mistake of thinking they had acquired a trivial fact from a newspaper, when actually the experimenters had supplied it (Schacter, Harbluk & McLachlan, 1984, https://scholar.harvard.edu/files/schacterlab/files/schacterharblukmclachlan1984.pdf).

While commonplace, the storage of "facts" and the source of those facts don't always match up. In most cases it is simply no big deal. There have been, however, situations where misattribution of a memory resulted in an arrest for crimes not committed. This is where a witness or victim recalls the trauma of an event but misattributes the face of the purported attacker from some other memory source. There have been cases of what was thought to be sexual abuse that when investigated by a therapist turn out to have been an abduction event.

The perpetrator, thought to be human, certainly, and possibly even a known person or relative, turned out to be a misattribution of memory. The subject, while under the care of a *trained* hypnotherapist, might recall the image of an alien invasive intrusion instead of the expected rational explanation of having a human attacker rather than a nonhuman one.

5. Suggestibility

Suggestibility refers to an individual's tendency to incorporate faulty or misleading information from outside sources into their personal recollections at a later date. For example, a group of Dutch psychologists, ten months after the noted crash of an El Al cargo plane into an eleven-story building in 1992, polled university workers about what they remembered. They were asked one simple question: "Did you see the television film of the moment the plane hit the apartment building?"

About 55 percent said yes, they had seen footage of the plane plowing into the building. In a later poll, two-thirds said yes to seeing it. The problem with this was that there was never any footage of the moment the plane hit the building. It had not been caught on film. People had heard about it and had seen footage of the aftermath of it but never saw the plane hit the building—although it was blatantly implied during the question that it had been broadcast on TV, it never happened.

After the horrible attacks on 9/11 of the Twin Towers in New York City, now well over fifteen years ago, we suspect the same type of study could have been done. The image of the plane hitting the second tower was shown on TV too many times to count and is certainly burned into our memory, but most of us were not there.

The suggestibility and memory we are talking about involve how the brain reassembles the memory and whether it uses the correct facts versus the implied facts that have been inputted. Anytime hypnotic regression is used to investigate a possible alien abduction, suggestibility and the use of hypnotic regression become a topic for conversation.

An investigator who might accidentally ask a leading question of a witness or make implications can contribute to steering the direction of the testimony and result in inaccurate information. This does not always mean the witness will have false memories, just that the info could be tainted.

Please understand that many people are easily suggestible without ever being put into a relaxed or regressive state. Once induced into that state, they are of an even more suggestible nature. If the person is put into a regressive state and is asked leading questions, the witness may in some way want to please the investigator and go in that implied direction of the testimony. There is a possibility that unintended memory fabrication by witnesses could create false memories upon retrieval at a later date.

Many studies have been done to show misleading information fed to us every day from other people making suggestive statements—in the media, video, and the written word used to implant incorrect information. "If you hear a lie enough times, you will start to believe it." Control by suggestibility is done every day (the act of suggesting, not suggestibility of memory). The news media and the advertising world abound with it. The news isn't the news anymore. It's more like an opinion that leans one way or the other, and anyone who is suggestible watching it can be swayed to that opinion. Another form of control, but not along the original lines of this section.

Many people have a certain level of suggestibility. A stage hypnotist will look for signs of suggestibility in individuals in the audience by how they react to him. These are the people he may choose for the show, people he will have suggestive control over during the performance. The people paying admission are not there to see the stage hypnotist; they are there to see other individuals "controlled" by him and to have a good time.

Memory suggestibility is kind of related to misattribution, but it usually has a driving force, a suggestibility that may steer the supposed memory into a confabulation. Memories of the past are often influenced by the manner in which they are recalled. When subtle and sometimes not so subtle emphasis is placed on certain aspects of memory during an investigation, a specific memory may be created or fabricated internally by someone of high suggestibility, which has nothing to do with true recollection.

For example, a stage hypnotist putting on a show in a well-air-conditioned lounge in Las Vegas may pick a suggestible subject from the floor of the show and suggest to him that the A/C has failed, and that it is getting very hot inside. You might see the man loosen his tie and start to perspire profusely. Getting hotter, he may take off his jacket and request some water. The subject is neither hot nor parched but believes he is during his participation, because of his level of suggestibility and being induced into a relaxed state.

6. Bias

Bias refers to the distorting influences of present-day knowledge, personal feelings, and beliefs upon recollection of experiences from one's past. Bias is similar to suggestibility in that one's current worldview may affect how past events are reassembled for recall. Basically, the way you were then is not always the way you are now.

Consistency bias has to do with memories of past attitudes distorted to be like your current attitudes. In 1986, Greg Markus from the University of Michigan used data collected about personal opinions from two generations. The study consisted of two points in time, 1973 and 1982. There were 898 parents along with 1,135 of their children participating, giving their attitudes toward common issues of 1973, such as legal issues of marijuana use or gender equality.

Polled again in 1982, both parents and their children had become more conservative as they aged. When asked to think back to how they reported their beliefs from almost a decade previous, only about a third of the people correctly recalled their political positions from 1973. Another third recalled their position incorrectly. The last third polled were somewhere in between (Markus 1986).

Everything that we do, think, or experience is affected by past thoughts and things that have already happened to us. Memory is what makes us who we are. As a result, we can't help but put our own personal spin on our memories. Most individuals recall the past in a self-enhancing way. (For example, I am much grander in my own mind than in anyone else's.) It's like the fisherman whose fish story gets bigger and bigger over time.

Abductees are affected by bias as well in some cases by putting their own spin on the memories, perhaps to make them more palatable. In one way it is probably a protective mechanism of the psyche to adjust for a trauma.

Here is an example: the abduction of Betty Andreasson. On the night of January 25, 1967, Betty was working in her kitchen while her seven children and both her parents were in the living room. At about 6:30 p.m., the lights in the house briefly blinked out, and a red light began to beam through the kitchen window. Betty's father ran into the kitchen to look out the window to see what was causing the red light. To his amazement he saw five strange-looking beings coming toward the house. The beings entered the house by walking right through the wooden door! (We see this type of entrance and exit time and time again, where the beings just float through a solid object, and we will cover this in a later chapter.)

Everyone in the whole family was suddenly put into a state of suspended animation, just frozen in place. One of the beings began to make telepathic communication with Betty (always a part of the scenario). Betty said that all the beings had bulbous, pear-shaped heads, wide eyes, and small ears and noses. They had the typical slit for a mouth that never moved, though they were able to communicate through telepathy.

Betty would later recall that, while she was frightened, she felt a sense of calm, even friendship toward the beings (possible alien manipulation of thought to control subject). Betty was taken outside to a small craft, your typical 20-foot saucer. She believes it joined a mother ship, where she underwent the typical physical examination during an abduction, and then had what she equates to a kind of religious experience. She was taken before an enormous door, where she was to meet "the One." Upon the door opening, there was extremely bright light, and Betty had what appeared to her to be an out-of-body experience, where her physical body just stood there, and her ethereal body went through the door to see "the One."

Betty's case involved twelve months of investigation. UFO investigator Ray Fowler and his team of professionals enlisted the service of a hypnotist and a medical doctor trained in psychiatry. Betty was given a character reference check, two lie-detector tests, a psychiatric review, and an excruciating fourteen sessions of regressive hypnosis.

They tried repeatedly through hypnotic regression to get further information about her experience beyond the door with "the One," but to no avail. She told them repeatedly that she could not tell them anything about it except that "their father loves everyone."

Before this bizarre happening, Betty had little knowledge of UFOs, and, being a devoted Christian, she believed that the abduction had a religious meaning. It would be later before she began to view the abduction as alien in nature (Fowler 1979).

Several things come to mind here. Did Betty's religious bias determine her experience? Did the alien beings have more control over Betty by creating a religious-type experience for her? This is certainly an atypical abduction experience. While Ray Fowler and his team conducted an exhaustive investigation, hypnotic regression was still not the end-all to giving answers to the questions the team asked.

Betty had also stated that she felt the aliens had hypnotized her to forget and to remember at a later time. Did the aliens have a more effective method of hypnotizing Betty? To the point that Fowler's attempts were thwarted?

The bias created by one's attitude certainly has an effect. It is much more pleasing to believe that you are part of saving the world for the good of everyone than to believe that you are a breeding chamber for a hybrid race to overtake us. We know we will get flak for that statement, but we've heard it stated by abductees both ways and everywhere in between. Everyone has a spin or bias to cope with the experience. Good or bad.

One remaining point about bias we would like to make: Memories encoded while a person was feeling a certain level of heightened arousal and a certain type of emotion come to mind more quickly when a person is in a similar mood. A rape victim may have a hard time becoming intimate with a spouse after the fact, due to the linking of a negative sexual bias with what should be a pleasant one.

An abductee who experiences a sexual encounter may have the same type of linked bias and associated feelings. Feelings of remorse or guilt from a forced sexual encounter to harvest eggs or sperm are common.

"Rose-tinted specs: Remember how wonderful things were in the olden days? It wasn't that good, trust us; nostalgia isn't what it used to be" (PSYBLOG).

7. Persistence

It is the persistence of memories involving the unwanted recall of information that is of a disturbing nature. The unwanted recall can range from something stupid you did in public that you would just as soon forget, to a truly traumatic experience that will not go away. A persistently traumatic recall can lead to the formation of phobias, posttraumatic stress disorder, and even suicide in especially disturbing and intrusive instances, all of which the alien abduction phenomenon has seen.

1. Transience:	Decreasing accessibility of memory over time
2. Absentmindedness:	Lapses of attention that result in forgetting (ADDers know this one)
3. Blocking:	Information is present but temporarily inaccessible.
4. Misattribution:	Memories are attributed to an incorrect source.
5. Suggestibility:	Implanted memories about things that never occurred
6. Bias:	Current knowledge and beliefs distort our memories of the past.
7. Persistence:	Unwanted recollections that we can never forget

From the book *The Seven Sins of Memory* by Daniel L. Schacter, 2001.

Among other types of memories besides short term and long term are forgotten memories, repressed memories, and screened memories. Some of these memories may be of a nature that we do not wish to remember. Unfortunately, we don't always have a choice.

This really isn't a scientific analogy, but we think you will get the point. How many times have you gone to the store to buy some things, and when you got there, you couldn't remember everything you wanted? How many times have you come across a friend or acquaintance whom you haven't seen in a while and have forgotten his or her name? Did you ever, in the middle of a conversation, stop and announce to the person you are talking to that "I just had something to say and forgot; it was just on the tip of my tongue and now it's gone." Now it really wasn't on the tip of your tongue, but it was stored somewhere in your brain's memory banks, and now it seems to be gone. Or have you ever been interrupted, and when you went back to the conversation, you forgot what you were talking about? These things are usually caused by distractions. You get sidetracked, and your mind simply displaces your thought. Any of you ADDers out there know what we're talking about. Attention deficit disorder can wreak havoc on your short-term memory. No big deal; it comes back to you . . . eventually.

It usually requires a trigger event such as returning to the room in which you had the original thought or returning to the same task at hand that prompted the idea in the first place—then it all comes flooding back like the flick of a switch.

Stresses of everyday life get the best of all of us sometimes. Most of the time with forgotten memories, it's just a question of focus, proper sleep, and proper diet, and it's not something your mind is trying to hide from you!

Repressed Memories

Repressed memory is a concept used to describe a significant traumatic memory that has become unavailable for the memory process to recall. Due to traumatic experiences, the brain may be motivated to block out certain memories that are painful or traumatic until a time when stress is at a lower level. (Note: Relaxation techniques up to and including hypnotic induction and regression are effective tools for memory retrieval due to lowering stress levels.)

Repressed memory is not the same as amnesia, which is a term for any instance in which memories either are not stored in the first place (such as with traumatic head injuries when short-term memory does not transfer to long-term memory) or are forgotten (see the "Amnesia" entry in *Encyclopedia of Psychology*, published by the American Psychological Association).

In psychology, the term "repressed memory" is used to describe memories that have been dissociated from awareness, as well as those that have been repressed without dissociation. Repressed-memory syndrome, the clinical term used to describe repressed memories, is often compared to psychogenic amnesia. Psychogenic amnesia is characterized by the sudden loss of one's own autobiographical memory for a period of time ranging from hours to years (Leong, Stephanie, Wendi Waits, and Carroll Diebold [2006]. "Dissociative Amnesia and DSM-IV-TR Cluster C Personality Traits." *Psychiatry [Edgmont]* 3, no. 1. [2006] January; 3[1]: 51–55. PMCID: PMC2990548).

These gaps involve an inability to recall personal information, even to the extent of not knowing who you are or where you live. Or even memories of your family may be blocked, with one not being able to remember a spouse or children.

Here is an example of a repressed memory involving a couple who lived in Ticonderoga, New York, which we discussed earlier; the ones who took the video of a UFO and did not remember or discuss it for eight days. What happened to them to cause them to forget such an event? Could it have been that the events that happened after the videotaping, which could not be remembered for years, had been so traumatic that they just blocked it out of their minds? Or were the traumatic memories possibly put someplace in their minds so deep that they could not find them until assisted?

The existence of repressed memories is a controversial topic in psychology; some studies have concluded that it can occur in victims of trauma (e.g., war, horrific accidents, alien abduction), while others dispute it. According to the American Psychological Association, it is not currently possible to distinguish a true repressed memory from a false one without corroborating evidence ("Questions and Answers about Memories of Childhood Abuse," www.apa.org/topics/trauma/memories).

If the repressed memory is indeed of a real event, the next question is, What is the mechanism of the repression? Is the source of the repression coming from the individual as a method of coping with a traumatic memory, or is the repression an induced repression, possibly meaning that the memory is being blocked by some outside source?

If an alien technology could learn enough about our body functions—and God knows they abducted possibly a few million humans by this point if polls and statistics are correct—they sure as hell should have our bodily functions figured out. So, let's assume that they have and they can induce or control hormones in the brain to inhibit memory captured in the immediate memory, so it never gets transported to the hippocampus to be put in short-term memory.

The problem with that is that the memory does get captured, because it comes out as flashbacks later, on its own or through hypnotic regression. So it is in there, just initially unfiled or being filtered. Or maybe the chemical-hormonal control they have of the victim has only a limited effect, and they use it just to get through the basic abduction and really don't care if it comes out later with the abductee or not. After all, the abductee has no choice in the matter, right? The entities will find you anywhere and at any time, no matter who or how many people are around you. I (Bob) had one woman who was taken from a group of over twenty people standing in a field.

False Memories

Sometimes the brain gets confused as to what is real and what is confabulated or a construct of the mind. Someone who is put into an altered state of consciousness by a trained professional hypnotherapist can be susceptible to suggestions because they have more of a direct link to the subconscious mind, and the filtering system is less enforced than with the conscious mind.

However, and I (Bob) have seen this for myself, sometimes when a person is put under into a regressive state, the person inducing the regression makes a suggestible test question to see if the person being regressed is going to confabulate or go against the suggestion or leading test question. I will give an example. A very common occurrence for an abductee aboard a craft is to be put onto an examination table. The table is of a monopedestal design coming up from the floor of the craft, like it is all one piece. The common test question is to ask how many legs are on the table. We know from thousands of reports at this point that the table is the monopedestal design that we mentioned. If the person is prone to confabulate, they will give you the expected number of legs on a table and answer four legs. A subject who is not going to confabulate and is having an accurate memory may well correct the questioner, who may be asking a purposely leading question as a test for confabulation and say, "No, that is not how it was; it was like this."

One of our favorites stories involved Budd Hopkins: He would test his subjects with a made-up word and ask if they had heard the aliens say this word. If the subject said, "No, never heard that word, and besides the aliens don't talk," then you knew you were in good shape and could keep confabulation to a minimum with very carefully asked questions. You would usually ask questions that had no implied direction and were of a very mundane nature, where the abductee would likely answer just the opposite of someone who wasn't an abductee in some cases.

For example:

Question: Did you believe in Santa Claus and the Easter Bunny when you were a child?

Answer: Yes.

Question: Did you have any imaginary friends when you were little?

Answer: They weren't my friends!

Question: Who wasn't your friends?

Answer: The little scary people.

Question: Why weren't they your friends?

Answer: They hurt my nose and made me bleed.

This is a perfect example of normal questions taking a wild turn. Most people we have worked with have had a great many conscious memories. Hypnotic regression is best left to the professionals, who are clinically trained. That way, someone who might be fantasy prone will not have the possibility of having a false memory planted at the hands of someone with good intentions but a poorly designed question. Number-one rule: Do no harm to the people you are trying to help. A person wanting to investigate some anomalous experience in their life should have total control and choice in the matter. It's definitely not for everybody.

The Other Side of the Coin

Speaking of false memories, who is to say that the aliens haven't implanted false memories on purpose to keep their clandestine efforts covert? If they are as adept at manipulation as suggested, why would they not combine erasing or covering of memories with false ones or screened memories?

What about abductions that had a military presence? Is our military beyond being involved with operations to install false memories or intimidation of other military personnel? The CIA had a certain fondness for some of the psychotropic drugs such as LSD that they experimented with, unbeknown to the individual being the subject of the mind-altering experiments such as project MKULTRA that we discussed earlier under mind control.

Screened Memories

A screened memory is a memory that is not true. It is a fabrication. It may be a self-induced memory to replace a traumatic real event or it may be an implanted memory to trick the mind into believing something that someone else does not want you to recall.

Let us first examine the self-induced screened memory. One example of a self-induced memory might be the cover-up of an abuse by someone of greater authority, such as a parent or guardian. When a child is beaten and is told to lie about what happened for fear of reprisal, he or she will tell that lie enough times so that when questioned in the future, he or she may actually believe it happened that way—such as "I fell down a flight of steps, and that is how I broke my arm when I was ten years old." Many times, a sexual assault on a child may be the cause of the screened memory. Fear and threats are usually the leading factor for the internal mind cover-up. As has been proven all too many times in the hospitals and courts, not all accidents are the result of a real accident. As it can be said, not all reported claims of physical and sexual abuse were as reported.

Another cause of a screened memory is when a person deliberately sets out to basically brainwash someone. Some means that have been used to brainwash an individual are hypnosis, subliminal messages, sleep deprivation, isolation, and drugs, and the list can go on.

Hypnosis has been around for a long time. Now it is used mostly for entertainment and therapy. The use of hypnosis can be a powerful tool when used properly. It has been used to help people forget certain things that have traumatized them, such as seeing a life-changing event. Maybe it was being in an automobile accident where a loved one was killed. It could be used to help the witness accept the event and not let it consume him or her, so the person could get on with his or her life. Or maybe it was used to alleviate pain during surgery. Hypnosis is also used by entertainers. The hypnotist can relax and comfort you to the point where you go into a deep, relaxing state of consciousness. You are never unconscious. He (the hypnotist) may make you do certain things that you wouldn't typically do, for fear of ridicule, such as bark like a dog on command or walk like a duck. They may even be able to make you forget your own name or where you live, although this is usually only a temporary state of mind. And if they could remove a part of your memory, what would stop them from being able to input a false memory? Would it be possible to remove all memory of what happened to you on a certain night and replace it with a whole new memory that never really happened?

Subliminal messages work. How many times have you gone to the store to buy something and bought something you didn't intend to? Advertisers are the experts at this. Did you ever buy anything you really had no need for but just had to have a product because you thought someday you might need it? Watching commercials on TV seems like a boring thing while waiting for the show you want to see to come back on; you may not even be paying attention to the commercial, but you have been looking at it. What you were able to see was what the advertiser wanted you to know and pay attention to and remember. What the advertiser didn't want you to see was a very quick flash of a word or a product many times on the screen, so fast that you think you didn't see anything . . . but it was there. Your subconscious saw the flash, and when seen enough times by you, the duped viewer, it became a necessary item when you saw it again in a store. Usually when you get home, you wonder, "Why did I buy that?" Repetition and hidden messages are how that works. This is why during the most watched annual event in any year, the Super Bowl, so many millions of dollars are charged just for a thirty-second advertisement. A lot of people who are not football fans watch the Super Bowl just for the commercials, and so the advertisers make the most of this opportunity and come up with the most-memorable ads. This is *their* Super Bowl also.

Sleep deprivation and other techniques have been used either alone or in conjunction with other means to get control of someone, either as torture as with a captured enemy soldier or by an illegal crime organization to elicit information. This can also be used to make a person forget what they know, or believe what is expected of them to know.

A good example of how a screen memory and control might work is shown in the movie *The Manchurian Candidate*. Two versions of this movie were made, and although it was a Hollywood product, the concept does seem plausible. The movie uses the idea of a soldier who when captured is tortured to weaken his resistance and then hypnotized to remember his military past differently than it was. He is then programmed, upon a command, to assassinate a politician so he could replace him and then act as a puppet to do the bidding of his controller.

At the beginning of this book we told of a man and his wife who were driving along a highway (New York State Thruway). This man relayed how he believed he was controlled to forget his enthusiasm to take a picture of a UFO landing alongside the road, near his car. This witness has mentioned the control that the aliens had over him numerous times, both this time and other times of abduction; he believes that the aliens have such control that you think that whatever you are being controlled into doing are normal acts and not controlled ones. He said that they make you believe that what you do is what you want to do, and not that they are instructing you to do it. The control is so great that if they wanted you to pick up a gun and shoot someone, you would do it because you believe that you want to do it, and it is the right thing to do. He also said he feels that they might even be able to make you commit suicide. Interesting thought. That of course remains to be proven but is scary nonetheless.

The study of hypnosis tells you that nobody is capable of doing something that they do not really want to do, but what if the aliens are using another means of control or a hypnosis technique that makes you think you want to do what they want? Could it be possible to hypnotize someone, perhaps with the use of drugs, into believing that they want to do something that they ordinarily wouldn't do? Can a person be made to believe that he or she would believe that something is totally their own idea, while really being used as a pawn and being instructed in their behaviors?

Attempts at Memory Retrieval

Memory retrieval works better when the subject is in a relaxed state. No pressure to perform, no expectations. Calm, reclined, and quiet. No adrenaline to screw it up. No other thoughts flooding in. No other distractions.

When a memory is seemingly lost, how can you retrieve it? One method to recall a name of a person or place, as we talked about in blocking and tip-of-the-tongue stuff, is the alphabet method. This is where you start at the letter *A* and work your way down to *Z* to see if a clue will pop up at you. If you get a gut feeling of the beginning letter, sometimes the name will jump out and strike you. Sometimes that works and sometimes that isn't enough.

Another way might be through association. Associate the person with some other fact held within your memory, such as what they do for a living, where they live, or what their spouse's name is. Look for clues to forge a new pathway for your memory to be assembled and come forward.

Say you remember a particular comedic team from a movie but you can only remember one of the names. Budd Abbott is the name you remember, but who was his partner? You play with the name of Abbott and try to picture what he looked like and then who was with him. Maybe you do the alphabet method on the name, or possibly you can remember a scene from a movie and part of the dialogue. Sooner or later the name of the other comedian will pop up because Abbott mentions it quite frequently. Lou! That's it—his name was Lou, but what was his last name? Think now, Lou what? Abbott and . . . Costello. That's it, Abbott and Costello.

Let's assume you are trying to recall an event. Maybe it was a particular play in a football game. You start at the point that made you think of the play and then, step by step, describe each move. Make it seem like a video you are replaying in your mind. Like the movie you tried to remember with Abbott and Costello, you remember parts of the movie and replay it in your head till the next scene just appears, and you then go on to the next scene.

Sometimes, however, none of the memory tricks will work, and you must go to outside help. If someone else was with you, you may ask the other person for a reminder of what happened. All you need is one successful trigger word to get recall going.

If nobody was with you and you can't recall, and it is important information you are trying to retrieve, such as what happened during an alien abduction, you may start by contacting a doctor. He or she may refer you to a specialist.

In the case of a suspected alien abduction, you may contact an organization like the Mutual UFO Network. Sometimes just talking with a trained investigator, who knows how to ask the appropriate questions, can jar loose memories without any use of hypnosis. Remember, just because you "think" you may have experienced an abduction does not make it so. Vivid dreams or drug reactions can seem very real too. Let a professional help sort it out.

Ultimately, it is your determination if you have experienced an abduction or not. Sometimes to get through tough mental blocks you may have to use the services of a trained and board-certified hypnotherapist. The most important aspect of using a hypnotherapist is that the person is experienced in this type of regressive hypnosis and does not lead the person or ask questions that might cause the abductee to remember things that didn't happen.

MUFON can supply a list of hypnotherapists who are familiar with the abduction scenario. One last very important thing about memory retrieval that you should be sure to consider. Be cautious of what you wish for. Hidden memories can affect your life in untold ways. Sometimes, not knowing is better than knowing. Every person is different. If you do regression and it turns out to be nothing, great! It's a win, all the way around.

If you do a regression and it turns out to be traumatic and real, you can't put the genie back in the bottle or unlearn a stark truth about your life that affects you and everyone else in it. We only recommend hypnotic regression if the memories or flashbacks become disturbing to your everyday life. If you are losing sleep, you can't work, you are showing signs of posttraumatic stress disorder, or it is causing problems at home, then it might be time to consult a certified hypnotherapist familiar with the problem for help.

PTSD symptoms include the following:

- Alcohol or drug problems: Some people drink to get away from problems. Abductees are no different.
- Anger and irritability
- Chronic pain
- Confusion
- Difficulty concentrating
- Dizziness
- Eating problems
- Feeling on edge
- Hypervigilance: Feeling like you're constantly on guard. Fairly common with abductees.

- Feelings of hopelessness: You may feel hopeless when facing tough times in your life, but there are other ways to overcome your problems. Help is out there.
- Flashbacks: The feeling of reliving a traumatic experience. Really common with abductees.
- Gambling
- Guilt: as we have discussed with abduction and sexual encounters with other abductees
- Headaches: These might be a result of stress, tension, injury, or illness.
- Loss of interest or pleasure: Loss of interest or pleasure in things can affect your relationships, work, and activities.
- Nightmares: very common with abductees
- Noise or light irritation: Abductees often see and hear things that others do not.
- Reckless behavior
- Relationship problems: Can be a big one. Spouses often blame you for the aliens showing up.
- Social withdrawal/isolation: Feeling like you are alone and no one else will understand. Seeking out an abduction group meeting helps a lot.
- Stress and anxiety: kind of goes without saying
- Trouble sleeping: The whole "trying to sleep with one eye open" sort of thing, waiting

12

HOW COME SOME PEOPLE CAN SEE UFOs AND SOME CAN'T?

SOME PEOPLE WILL NEVER SEE A UFO because it's just a case of never looking up. They will never enjoy all the natural phenomena that there are to see.

Some are more than casual observers of the sky and see Venus, shooting stars, sun dogs, or rainbows. Still others see interesting and unknown things because they are always looking up. They might become occasional night gazers, having sky watches with telescopes and a thermos of hot coffee and camaraderie. They spend nights catching meteor showers, occasional comets, the moon's lunar surface, and the planets in our solar system. Amateur astronomers are always looking at the heavens.

While many professional astronomers have seen the wonders of the heavens, they may have never seen a UFO. Chance plays a part, as does their field of sight being so small and focal distances being so great; they wouldn't see a plane, either, except for maybe an unfocused flash as it passed in front of the lenses. The only reason we mention this is that we have heard the argument that there cannot be UFOs because astronomers never see them. Debunkers, "ya gotta love 'em."

Pilots, on the other hand, have been seeing UFOs since the 1940s. Commercial pilots see UFOs but come forth with few public reports due to the flack that comes with reporting such phenomena. Coined Foo Fighters during World War II, military pilots became good information sources for sightings, although usually in confidence. We personally have talked with

US Air Force fighter pilots off the record about close encounters they have experienced. Numerous military pilots have had these kinds of encounters. One pilot assured me that he could punch a hole in one, if he could ever catch one to do so. This pilot flew an F-16 Fighting Falcon with a top advertised speed of around 1,600 mph! He was on an intercept course, and when he made radar contact with it, it just blew away from him like he was going backward. He then proceeded with some explicative regarding the unknown object's speed. He never knew any more because his plane was stripped of hard radar data upon landing. Gun cameras were removed too, although he never got close enough for a visual.

Kenneth Arnold

On June 24, 1947, private pilot Kenneth Arnold claimed he spotted a string of nine shiny unidentified flying objects flying past Mount Rainier in the state of Washington. Clocking how long it took the objects to fly between the mountains peaks showed them to be flying at a then-unheard-of supersonic speed of 1,200 miles an hour. This was the first postwar sighting and garnered nationwide news coverage. Arnold's description of the objects also led to the press quickly coining the terms "flying saucer" or "flying disc."

Captain Thomas F. Mantell

Captain Thomas F. Mantell was a 25-year-old Kentucky Air National Guard pilot, and on January 7, 1948, he died while in pursuit of a supposed UFO. The incident was among the most publicized early UFO reports. Mantell was an experienced pilot who had been honored for his part in the Battle of Normandy during World War II.

Kentucky State Highway Patrol received reports of an unusual westbound aerial circular object, 250 to 300 feet in diameter. Observers at Clinton County Army Air Field in Ohio described the object "as having the appearance of a flaming red cone trailing a gaseous green mist" and observed the object for around thirty-five minutes (I just hate those meteors that hang around for thirty-five minutes and change course). Four P-51 Mustangs of C Flight were already in the air, one piloted by Mantell, and they were told to approach the object. Sgt. Blackwell was in radio communication with the pilots throughout the event. Mantell continued to climb past his ceiling, with no oxygen onboard, chasing the UFO, which he reported as being metallic and huge. According to the air force, once Mantell passed 25,000 feet, he supposedly blacked out from the lack of oxygen, and his plane began spiraling back toward the ground. A witness later reported Mantell's Mustang in a circling descent. His plane crashed at a farm on the Tennessee-Kentucky state line.

Pilots do not seem to have a problem seeing UFOs. Why could someone on the street be able to see an unknown craft hovering, and someone else on the same street not be able to see the craft? Perhaps it is the mode of operations they are engaged in that determines whether a person can see them or not.

Sometimes UFOs show up in highly populated areas, yet no one seems to notice except for just a few. Is this because no one is paying attention or because of some type of stealth? Or is it something else? Are the entities in the craft only allowing a certain few to see them somehow?

Our own stealth aircraft, such as the F-117 Nighthawk or B2 Spirit, are flat black in color and, with the exception of air shows, fly mostly at night. Our military has experimented with daytime aircraft color schemes that are light blue on the bottom and dark camouflage patterns on the top to blend with the ground. The military has been experimenting with and now probably has craft that use phased-array optics (PAO) that implement active camouflage, not by producing a two-dimensional image of background scenery on an object, but by computational holography to produce a three-dimensional hologram of background scenery on an object to be concealed. They are reported to have small panels that can change color like a huge mosaic to blend into the background and even produce patterns on the skin of the craft to remain less detectable to the naked eye, as well as thermal camouflage to hide infrared heat signatures.

Dr. David R. Smith is currently the William Bevan Professor of the Department of Electrical and Computer Engineering at Duke University, and director of the Center for Metamaterial and Integrated Plasmonics. He is working on developing what he calls metamaterials. Electromagnetic metamaterials are artificially structured materials that are designed to interact with and control electromagnetic waves. Electromagnetic waves might be any type of wave in the electromagnetic spectrum. He has developed a material that is invisible to microwaves. Microwaves are not visible light but are part of the electromagnetic spectrum between radio waves and infrared. Microwaves are absorbed at varying degrees into matter. As waves are absorbed, heat is generated, as is evident by your cold cup of coffee being reheated or your microwave dinner becoming piping hot through the excitation of water molecules.

This new material allows microwaves to bend around it and or split and rejoin on the opposite side of the material. The wave is not stopped or absorbed. Bottom line, they have shown the principle of invisibility at microwave frequency. The obvious next step is creating material that will bend visible light to achieve invisibility in the visible spectrum.

Alien stealth technology might be so much different than ours to the point that the craft is not really there at all. We know how that sounds, and we will get into that soon, but for now let's look at the fact that many, if not most, UFO reports include the description of some type of ionizing luminous glow on the skin of the craft that has the whole craft glowing luminously and easy to see—or there's a bright lighting array that is blinking variously colored lights. Some are reported with lights being where engine exhaust might be, on the end of the craft, while others have flashing strobe lights around the perimeter of a sphere or circular craft—again, nothing like the FAA-required wing lights or belly strobes on our conventional aircraft, but very easy to see.

An unidentified craft with nothing short of spectacular blinding lighting displays or maneuvers (or both), seeming to attract attention, sometimes in front of small crowds, does not sound to us like whoever it is doesn't want to be seen, at least by the chosen people viewing the display. We don't mean for that to sound so ominous, being the chosen, but it is what it is.

Back in the mid-eighties, in the Hudson Valley area of New York State, there was a sighting flap with over 7,000 documented UFO sightings. Someone or something did not care if it was seen. This was well documented by Philip Imbrogno in the book *Night Siege*.

And then, there are everyday people who see UFOs on a fairly regular basis. A small group of kids were playing basketball early one evening in a local park in Yonkers, New York. The sidewalks were filled with pedestrians, and the streets were filled with cars driving around. Everybody was going about their business. During the basketball game in the park, one of the kids noticed an unusual object flying slowly and low in the sky over the neighborhood. He brought it to the attention of the other kids playing, and they all stopped to look at the object. One kid said it was so low as it hovered above them that they could see most of the structure and the shape. The rest of the neighborhood paid no attention to the object, as if it wasn't there (personal interview).

At the 1993 MUFON International Symposium, held in Richmond, Virginia, abduction researcher Budd Hopkins told of the experience of an Australian couple he'd worked with regarding an abduction they'd had. To begin the tale, he showed a slide of a nice scene on a beach with a body of water. The photo showed the sand and the water, and a tree on the side of the image. What was missing from the photo, the woman explained to Budd while under a hypnotic regression, was that she and her two sons were supposed to be in the picture. They posed so that her husband could take the picture. When asked why they weren't in the picture, she explained, only through regression, because she did not know till then, that an object had floated in the air over them. Soon she and her two sons began to float up into the air toward the ball-shaped object. Her husband during this was still standing on the ground, posed to take the picture of them. When the abduction finished and the three were returned back to the beach, they were put in the same position they were originally. The husband was still in his original position, standing there, ready to take the picture. As it was, he did take the picture, but only after the wife and kids were gone; therefore, they were not in the photo. Budd asked about everybody else around them. How did they react to the UFO and the abduction and the husband just standing there, frozen, all that time in that position and not moving? The husband while under hypnotic regression said that the other people on the beach went about doing what they were doing before the incident. The surrounding people did not see him because the aliens had hidden him (the husband's words). He was hidden in plain sight, not moved but made invisible, as were the UFO and the abduction.

How is it that an object in the sky can be seen with the naked eye by one person, and another person who is nearby or within the visual range of the object cannot see it? Could it be that the object is not a solid object as it appears, and only a select few are given the image, like a select projection? Or could it be that some people are being manipulated and blocked from the sight of the object?

There are numerous reports where a witness watched an object fly across the sky, only to see it and then not see it. It vanished from sight right before their eyes. It is thought that the object has gone into a dimensional portal and vanished. It could also be that the object accelerated at such a high rate and jumped into "warp" speed, vanishing as in the old *Star Trek* TV series. The human eye can't focus on something moving or accelerating that fast, so it would appear to vanish.

One of us (Bob) had such an experience once on the New York State Thruway, which runs from New York City to Buffalo, New York.

I was heading west from Albany, heading to the Geneva exit, when I spotted a very bright oval light in the sky. It was late afternoon and the sun was backlighting some high clouds, and the object was between me and the clouds. First, I thought it was a plane on a flight path to Rochester Airport, but after many minutes of me watching this thing, it did not seem to get any farther away or deviate to the right or left. In fact, I seemed to be getting closer to it at just highway speed. Most aircraft must attain certain airspeed to stay in the sky. I was getting closer to it at 65 mph. This told me the object was not moving very fast, if at all. At its closest point to me, it appeared about the size of a halogen street lamp at about a quarter mile when suddenly it just vanished. This was daytime. I saw no structure or movement. It just seemed to implode and be gone! After bringing my car back under control from that shock, I realized I had been watching so closely that I overshot and missed my exit and was headed to Canandaigua! And no, I did not experience any missing time, just a missed exit.

Is it possible for the occupiers of an unidentified flying object to have a special connection to certain people that they can let some see them and others not? A man discussed in other parts of this book, Frank Soriano, says that there are times when he may be doing something or just relaxing around the house and he gets this thought in his head, like a message to go outside. When he does, within a few minutes, he will see an unidentified object fly across the sky. The object he has seen is not like any other object we have on Earth. This is discussed further in the chapter dealing with camera malfunctions. Thought manipulation and having strong, compulsive suggestions made internally seem to be common among abductees. Late-night drives in secluded areas, late-night walks to the woods, etc. We will get to thought manipulation later also. Let's get back to vanishing craft for now.

An explanation for the "now you see it, now you don't" vanishing craft that might be acceptable to skeptics and debunkers (because we do want to be fair) is that the internal structure of the human eye has a blind spot. All humans have this blind spot in their eye but are not aware of it. According to the *Encyclopedia Britannica*, the blind spot is a "small portion of the visual field of each eye that corresponds to the position of the optic disk (also known as the optic nerve head) within the retina. There are no photoreceptors (i.e., rods or cones) in the optic disk, and, therefore, there is no image detection in this area." Most people never know it's there, due to the brain adjusting and filling in the space, so it is undetected.

Another explanation might be the simple fact that they are not paying attention. Let's go back to the kids playing basketball in a local park while pedestrians are walking nearby and not seeing the hovering object. The basketball players are actively playing a game in which they are following a ball. The ball gets thrown up toward a basket and the players must look up at the ball to see if it goes in or to grab a rebound. They must look up. The nearby pedestrians are busy going about their life, paying attention to each other or watching traffic or anything other than looking up at the sky. They don't have to look up.

Now the concern here is that at one point the kids said it was hovering above them. Even though it was evening, a low-flying object would draw somebody's attention, and they would say something that would cause others to look up. The kids only spoke to themselves and did not yell out to others to look up. Nobody else apparently looked up and said anything either. Could these people have been "turned off" or their cognitive functions impaired and so they were not able to notice it?

Being Turned Off

There are numerous reports where someone who has been abducted out of their bed at night had tried to wake up a sleeping spouse next to them and had been unable to even with vigorous shaking. It seems almost as if they were in a coma and could not wake up. The same types of reports come from people traveling in the same automobile, with one of them, usually the one not being abducted, being frozen in some type of state and the abductee frantically trying to shake them to consciousness without success.

Superior Technology? Maybe. Superior Thinking? Maybe Not.

These alien creatures have become an embedded image in our modern culture. They have been given credit for doing some amazing things: ultrafast craft, beams of light that move objects, ability to move through solid objects like walls. Wow! Crazy stuff. One might get the feeling that they are vastly superior to our technology. Maybe.

More Than Stealth as We Know It

There are multiple reports of UFOs not being seen, except by people being affected by them. And there are reports of people who are being affected by the UFO that are not always being seen by anyone else. One must think that with so many instances of what seems to be invisibility, for lack of a better word, something along that line must be happening.

Out of Phase?

How much stealthier could you get than not really "being" there? Later we will get into the possibilities of multiverses, and that these beings and machines may not be coming from a faraway star system, but maybe somewhere much, much closer. Maybe close enough that they *are* here, just a molecular shift away at any time. Possibly they are in a parallel universe and travel back and forth by changing their "phase." It might go a long way into explaining ships that just vanish and beings that can walk through solid objects and then take one of us through the same wall.

Transitioning through Solids and Invisibility

With all the reports of people being taken from their homes or vehicles through solid objects, such as walls, closed windows, and windshields, etc., one must pause to ask how that could even be possible. In Budd Hopkins's book *Sight Unseen* (2003), Budd told the story of Katharina Wilson. He had worked with her abduction experience case starting back in 1987. Katharina is known to many in the field as a longtime abductee and supporter of those being abducted and looking for help and answers. She wrote of some of her experiences in her book *The Alien Jigsaw* in 1993 and has a website by the same name. One account of her abduction experiences was of interest to Budd as well as us.

In October 1995, Katharina had departed Oregon on a plane to speak at a UFO conference in Chicago. She began feeling odd just before landing at O'Hare International Airport. She was supposed to meet the promoter of the conference at the airport, but because of not feeling good, she had stopped by the restroom on the way to baggage pickup. Upon leaving the stall in the restroom, she soaped up her hands to wash at the sinks. The faucets were of the infrared sensor type that comes on as your hand movement triggers the water flow. Try as she might, she could not find a sink that would work to wash her hands. Other people in the bathroom were washing their hands, and Katharina would swoop in after someone else left their sink with the water running, only to have the water stop and not restart with her hands under it. Beginning to panic, she turned to a young woman who was finishing up at the sink and asked, "What am I, invisible?" The young woman turned in Katharina's direction but said nothing and proceeded to walk out of the restroom. Katharina spied the baby-changing area of the bathroom, which had normal faucets that you turned by hand, and went there to finish washing her hands.

Leaving the restroom, she continued to the baggage area. On the way she passed some pay phones and decided to call her husband as she had promised when she landed. The first thing her hubby said was "I see your plane was late getting to Chicago." She looked at her watch, which was still on Portland time, and the watch said 3:20. When she landed, it read 2:10! Now, after a very short trip to the restroom, she was disoriented and apparently had some missing time. She approached the baggage area to find that her suitcase and a box of materials for the presentation were the only things left and had just been removed by security. Everybody else was gone, as well as the rest of the luggage. She picked up her bags and saw the promoter and assistant staring out the window waiting. She approached them, and they looked stunned and said, "It's like you just appeared. Where did you come from?"

Where *did* she come from? While this experience proves nothing, it is intriguing considering the implication of not being seen by people who were present and the missing time experienced while in the restroom, suggesting that she may have been altered or taken out of phase to make her either invisible intentionally or as a byproduct of an abduction.

Understanding the Impossible: Regaining Our Feeling of Control through the Understanding of Quantum Science

An abduction experience subjects someone to alien science that borders on magic. It is so far outside our normal paradigm of thinking that it stuns and confuses. It adds to the terror and chaos of the situation because it is so far beyond any experience in our normal everyday lives as it is, and then you add being removed from your house via going through a solid object like your bedroom wall. Overwhelming strangeness causes disbelief of the experience, which may favor the aliens in keeping their abductions covert. Anyone who is not immersed in the research of this enigma does not see the wealth of information available to those who wish to see, respect, and study it. Granted, the information is largely anecdotal, but no different than most of the verbal testimony accepted in a court of law.

I've been (Bob) an abduction researcher since the early '90s. Jim has been a UFO investigator for over fifty years, with ten of those years as MUFON's state director for New York. Jim and I have over 100 combined abduction cases under our belts. We have studied hundreds of other abduction cases from the better-known researchers such as Dr. David Jacobs, Budd Hopkins, Ray Fowler, Yvonne Smith, Dr. John Carpenter, Mark Rodeghier, Ann Druffel, Thomas (Eddie) Bullard, and Dan Wright of MUFON.

Wright headed the Abduction Transcription Project (ATP) in 1994, which supplied 317 summarized transcripts of hypnosis sessions and interviews from ninety-five separate cases. This involved a huge amount of data to be studied. Wright concluded that "Numerous entity types have been visiting our planet with some regularity." Dan served as deputy director of MUFON, in charge of investigations from 1987 to 1992.

We are rich in information from the past seventy-plus years of close encounters and abductions. Before we get started in the science, let us cover some basics in theory and try to answer how the aliens do what they do to us with impunity, using what exists today. Use this as a tool to analyze experiences, to understand that what may be happening to you has a basis in understandable science, and that hope of regaining control that once was thought to be totally lost by those having dreaded abduction experiences may be regained.

13

SCIENTIFIC THEORY

SCIENTIFIC THEORY IS A SET OF PRINCIPLES that explain and predict phenomena. Scientists create scientific theories with the scientific method. Ideas are originally proposed as hypotheses and are tested for accuracy through observations and experiments. Once a hypothesis is verified, it becomes a theory.

So, a scientific hypothesis is not the same as a scientific theory.

The definition of a working hypothesis according to the *Collins English Dictionary* is a suggested explanation for a group of facts or phenomena, accepted as a basis for further verification. Scientific hypotheses are based on observations not satisfactorily yet explained by available scientific theories.

The formal scientific definition of theory is quite different from the everyday meaning of the word according to the United States National Academy of Sciences. It refers to a comprehensive explanation of some aspect of nature that is supported by a vast body of evidence. Many scientific theories are so well established that no new evidence is likely to alter them substantially. For example, no new evidence will demonstrate that the Earth does not orbit around the sun (heliocentric theory), or that living things are not made of cells (cellular theory), that matter is not composed of atoms (atomic theory). One of the most useful properties of scientific theories is that they can be used to make predictions about natural events or phenomena that have not yet been observed (National Academy of Sciences, *Science, Evolution, and Creationism*, Washington, DC: National Academies Press, 2005).

There are many reported observations made by abductees that can't normally be explained by common everyday science. Scientific minds are logical, and often their operating parameters are known to be very rigid. Something being studied must meet the strictest scientific criteria and must be able to be replicated by others, or it cannot become a scientific theory.

An old friend of ours, the late Mr. David Bodner of upstate New York, a fellow investigator for MUFON, had a passion for science. He often spent time trying to explain the true meaning of scientific methodology during investigations. Here is one of the hurdles of trying to apply our science to what is being reported by abductees: the fact that alien science may be hundreds, if not thousands, of years advanced from where our current science is now.

Getting mainstream science to take a hard look at what is being reported and attempting to apply known science to it is a tough road. It's easy to say that something isn't possible when your science and engineering may be a thousand years behind. In the 1480s, Leonardo da Vinci drew sketches of human-powered flying contraptions, but not until the last 200 years have we graduated from jumping off towers with man-made wings to manned space flight, back and forth to the International Space Station.

Theoretical physics may be the pathway to one day understanding the observations that abductees have reported for decades. Testimony from people claiming to have experienced a close encounter with a UFO or an entity from inside a craft has developed patterns right from the early reports, long before the internet existed to disseminate information on the subject, and even before the hundreds of books on the subject were written. Raw unadulterated data.

These patterned observations, while fantastic in nature, are where theoretic physics needs to start. Why theoretic physics? *Webster's Dictionary* states that theoretical physics is relating to what is possible or imagined rather than to what is known to be true or real. Mathematical models and abstractions are used to rationalize, explain, and predict phenomena.

We have developed several tools and, in some cases, enormous machines to test these mathematical models and predict outcomes.

Thinking Outside the Box: Fringe Science

In 1982, Steven I. Dutch wrote a paper titled "Notes on the Nature of Fringe Science." This paper identified three classifications of scientific ideas—center or mainstream science, frontier science, and fringe science—with mainstream scientists typically regarding fringe concepts as highly speculative or even strongly refuted. Really wild ideas may be considered beyond the fringe, or pseudoscientific" (Steven I. Dutch, *Journal of Geological Education* 30, no. 1 [1982]: 6–13). I have heard the term "pseudoscience" thrown around over the years by scientists outside the UFO investigative community. It is disheartening to be deemed not worthy of investigation based on someone's biased opinion. Trying to get someone of serious scientific qualifications to investigate UFO/abduction science was practically impossible, and we (the ufological community) had almost no financial backing to do so. Of course, when it comes right down to that terminology, we have heard the term "pseudoscience" used about the field of psychology too. Psychology has had some nebulous footings in the past, but that field's theories seem well established these days. (Probably something to do with the multibillion-dollar psychotropic drug industry, but that's another story. Hey, maybe they could make an anti-abduction drug! Yes, we are being totally facetious.)

Fringe science is not openly considered within the scientific community. It is often a place where scientific novelists such as Isaac Asimov, Ray Bradbury, or Arthur C. Clarke write speculative fiction from a scientific standpoint. While fictional concepts and interpretations of how future science, such as how some fantastic starship might move through space, do not yet exist, applying "fringed science" to it may lead the way to it becoming a reality.

The Big Bang theory was once thought to be fringe science, but it lasted long enough for more supportive evidence to come to light. Quantum physics is, I suppose you could say, a fringe science, to understand the most ancient and illusive properties of matter and energy in our universe. While the term "fringe" may be insulting to some, billions of dollars worldwide are spent on huge particle accelerator facilities to try to understand it. Fringe science abounds with uncertainty. The uncertainty of it is what causes mainstream science to keep it at arm's length. Ultimately, we believe it will supply all the theoretical answers to explain the observations made by abductees/experiencers.

Simple Wave Theory

In 1678, Christiaan Huygens worked on the wave theory of light—that all light is transmitted by waves. Light, also known as electromagnetic energy, has been measured traveling in a wave. In fact, any time you have observed light, it has been traveling in waves. In the year 1900, Max Planck, attempting to explain black-body radiation, suggested that although light was a wave, these waves could gain or lose energy only in finite amounts related to their frequency. Planck called these "lumps" of light energy "quanta" (from a Latin word for "how much"). In 1905, Albert Einstein used the idea of light quanta to explain the photoelectric effect and suggested that these light quanta had a "real" existence. These light particles were named photons in 1926 by Gilbert N. Lewis ("December 18, 1926: This Month in Physics History," *APS News* 21, no. 11 [December 2012]). By the way, if you have ever touched a flat, black surface on a hot sunny day, you have experienced black-body radiation, and if the calculator on your desk has not only a battery but a solar cell, you are having the "lumps" of light energy power your calculator. It is all around us.

So, in common with all types of electromagnetic radiation, including visible light, it is emitted and absorbed in tiny "lumps" or "packets" called photons, and exhibits properties of both waves and particles. This property is referred to as the wave-particle duality. This is where the uncertainty comes in. Light depends on how you are testing and measuring it before it decides if it is going to be a wave or a particle—like it has a mind of its own! Newtonian science says that it is *either* this or that. Quantum science says that it *is* this and that.

Quantum Physics

Everyone has heard the words "quantum physics" or "quantum mechanics" somewhere. If you are not into quantum science, you have no idea what it is or what it represents other than it must be something so lofty and complicated that you would not be able to understand it, even if you tried, so most people don't. You have just experienced a small example of it.

There was a time not that long ago that I (Bob) fit into that category myself, although I have always had a curiosity about it and have accumulated dozens of scientific books, many dealing with quantum theory. Upon trying to unravel the UFO control mysteries, I discovered that quantum physics might hold the key to these entities doing what they do to us. There is a wealth of information available in books and on the internet from reputable and reliable universities and laboratories about quantum science, for those who wish to learn more.

What we are going to attempt here in a nutshell is to simplify quantum sciences and make it understandable for anyone who wishes to read it. No crazy equations or anything, but more of a glancing blow of the topic to show a little bit of what it is and how it relates to the topic of aliens' control of humanity and our systems. The concepts are not so hard to understand as much as it is just different from what we are taught with conventional science, and of course while it affects us on a molecular level, it is not relatable to us in our daily lives for the most part. It is our belief that alien technology functions more on the quantum level, and this is what allows them to perform such puzzling feats and acts of control on us and our surroundings.

Most of conventional science is what we refer to as Newtonian science, brought about by Sir Isaac Newton and the printing of his book *Principia* in 1687 ("Mathematical Principles of Natural Philosophy"). Newton became a celebrity after that, and it was the birth of the Newtonian science that we have today, based on experiments dealing with cause and effect. Most science today is based on experiments where we do something (i.e., the cause) and a result happens (i.e., the effect), while we stand back and observe. Everything in the

Newtonian universe is reducible to its smallest pieces. We have broken our world down into smaller and smaller individual parts. We have continued to take the machine apart and have isolated everything right down to the individual pieces of the atom, but in doing so we have lost our ability to see how all the pieces work together.

Our crazy, busy lives have brought about a cognitive lacking, a starvation of the imagination, if you will, of how the machine might be assembled to function in a more nonlinear way. We lack new coherent models that would forge new relationships between the parts of the machine to form a new whole. A more unified whole. The biggest fear to some is that the tightly held Newtonian science cannot deal or is unwilling to make room for something other than cause-and-effect science. Quantum science is largely the opposite of the everyday linear science that starts at point A and goes in a linear line to point B and then to point C. Quantum science can mean that things can be at all points at the same time in a nonlinear fashion, such as nonlocality, quantum entanglement, and quantum superposition.

Newtonian science is totally relatable to everyone in their everyday lives. The physics they have come to know is demonstrable in everything we do. Gravity and mass make things have weight (some of us more than others); the mass of atoms that you call a table seems solid and hard; and all hot things eventually seem to cool, even if you must blow on your steaming mashed potatoes before eating a forkful.

A point we would like to make here is that there is plenty of room for Newtonian physics as well as quantum physics. One does not make the other one wrong, just different. What we must do is succeed in coming up with a grand unified theory (GUT) or the theory of everything. In physics, a *unified field theory* (Albert Einstein, "On the Generalized Theory of Gravitation," *Scientific American* 182, no. 4 [1950]: 13–17) allows all that is usually thought of as fundamental forces and elementary particles to be written in terms of a single field. There is no accepted unified field theory at this point, and thus it remains an open line of research. The term was coined by Albert Einstein, who attempted to unify the general theory of relativity with electromagnetism, hoping to recover an approximation for quantum theory.

A grand unified theory is a model in particle physics in which at high energy, the three primary nuclear forces—the electromagnetic, weak, and strong interactions—are merged into one single interaction and thus one unified constant. A "theory of everything" is closely related to unified field theory but differs by not requiring the basis of nature to be fields, and it also attempts to explain all physical constants of nature. It will require a melding of conventional and quantum physics to do so.

Quantum physics is outside our everyday experiential reach most of the time and is not easily demonstrated. The concepts require high-end mathematics and incredibly expensive and often-massive machines.

CERN and the Large Hadron Collider (LHC)

The European Organization for Nuclear Research, known as CERN, located in Geneva, Switzerland, is one of the world's largest centers for scientific research when it comes to particle physics. Enormous machines, such as the Large Hadron Collider, accelerate particles to within a hair of the speed of light, inside a 17-mile loop underground, and collide them with other particles inside huge underground detectors.

These detectors observe and record the results, making note of the different subatomic particles that splatter after the collision. It is a lot like doing an autopsy on a possum that has been run over by a truck; we get to see the inside parts of the particle as they scatter and change in millionths of a second. We would much rather slide a live possum through a CAT scanner and get a precise picture, without destroying it, but technology has not gotten to the point that we can do that on a subatomic-particle level—and may never do so, since our machines are made of the same particles themselves. That may be a barrier that we cannot break, unless of course we discover that there are even-smaller pieces to the puzzle. Everything else is up for grabs.

Brookhaven National Laboratory

Brookhaven National Laboratory (BNL) is a US National Laboratory located in Upton, New York, on Long Island. They have the Relativistic Heavy Ion Collider (RHIC), which was designed to research quark-gluon plasma ("RHIC / Relativistic Heavy Ion Collider"; www.Bnl.gov/rhic/).

Until 2008, it was the world's most powerful particle accelerator. The gluon (love the name) is the force carrying particles of the strong nuclear force. There are four known nuclear forces: strong nuclear forces, weak nuclear forces, gravity, and electromagnetism. Gluons glue the quarks (the smaller particles that make up protons, neutrons, muons, baryons, and mesons) together. The RHIC can create the extremely high temperatures needed to cause the quarks and gluons to mix fluidly into quark-gluon plasma.

In 2010, RHIC physicists published results of temperature measurements from earlier experiments, which concluded that temperatures in excess of 4 trillion Kelvin (7 trillion degrees Fahrenheit) had been achieved in gold ion collisions, and that these collision temperatures resulted in the breakdown of "normal matter" and the creation of the quark-gluon plasma (Dennis Overbye, "In Brookhaven Collider, Briefly Breaking a Law of Nature," *New York Times*, February 15, 2010; Anne Trafton, "Explained: Quark-Gluon Plasma," *MIT News*, June 9, 2010, news.mit.edu/2010/exp-quark-gluon-0609).

SLAC National Accelerator Laboratory

Stanford Linear Accelerator Center is a US Department of Energy national laboratory operated by Stanford University. Founded in 1962 as the Stanford Linear Accelerator Center, the main accelerator is 2 miles long—the longest linear accelerator in the world—and has been operational since 1966. It is an RF (radio frequency) linear accelerator that can accelerate electrons and positrons and is claimed to be "the world's straightest object" (Alan T. Saracevic, "Silicon Valley: It's Where Brains Meet Bucks," *San Francisco Chronicle*, October 23, 2005). The main accelerator is buried 30 feet belowground, and the aboveground klystron gallery on top of the beam line is the longest building in the United States, at a length of 1.9 miles (SLAC National Accelerator Laboratory).

FERMILAB

The laboratory was founded in 1967 as the National Accelerator Laboratory and is located just outside Batavia, Illinois. It was renamed in honor of Enrico Fermi in 1974. Fermilab's Tevatron was a landmark particle accelerator; at 3.9 miles (6.3 km) in circumference, it was the world's second-largest energy particle accelerator at the time, with only CERN's Large Hadron Collider being larger, until being shut down on September 30, 2011.

It accelerates protons, delivers protons for antiproton production, and accelerates antiprotons coming from the antiproton source. Traveling at almost the speed of light, protons and antiprotons circle the Tevatron in opposite directions. Physicists coordinate the beams so that they collide at the centers of two 5,000-ton detectors, DØ and CDF, inside the Tevatron tunnel, revealing the innermost workings and pieces of the particle-antiparticle collision. The next step could be matter-antimatter annihilation, which could result in enormous energy release potential.

Sandia National Laboratories

Sandia National Laboratories in Albuquerque, New Mexico, has what they call the "Z" machine. It is the largest X-ray generator in the world and is used to test materials under extreme conditions of high temperature and pressure. The "Z" machine fires a huge electromagnetic pulse to the tune of 20 million amperes over a period of not more than 100 nanoseconds. This puts its output at 290 terawatts, which is enough to create enough heat and pressure to study nuclear fusion. To put this into everyday terms, picture producing about eighty times the world's electrical power output with a bank of Marx generators, which slowly builds up a charge into one blast that is over in 70 nanoseconds. What can this do? In 2003, it caused fusion of a small amount of deuterium, an isotope of hydrogen: nuclear fusion in a lab—a feat we take for granted when we look at the sun. The machine has created maximum internal temperatures of 6.6 billion degrees Fahrenheit. The "Z" machine can also accelerate small metal plates to a speed of 34 kilometers a second! For all of you metrically challenged folks, like ourselves, that's a little over 21 miles per second. The feats of the "Z" machine go on and on.

You may wonder what a brief description of these facilities has to do with a book on UFOs or the topic of alien abduction. You might question why scientific particle facilities belong in a book about the alien control over humans and their systems. People who have experienced different forms of control by these entities are so perplexed by the events that they witness that they find it hard to believe themselves. Some of the reported experiences border more either on magic or delusion than on our known reality.

The alien technology likely functions on physics that we have yet to discover or understand, but these facilities are studying the quantum subatomic particles that are likely involved with the control that these people are experiencing. You don't need to care or understand the facilities or the physics behind it all. But knowing that we are on the right track to understanding these unknown physics and the particles brings hope that this understanding will someday have solid footing within the scientific community, and maybe the ability even to wrestle control back from these entities that seem to plague certain individuals.

QUANTUM MECHANICS
I'VE HEARD OF IT, BUT WHAT IS IT?

Quantum mechanics is a subset of quantum physics that explains the physical behaviors at the atomic and subatomic levels. It is the study of the infinitely small. It all began with the idea that matter consisted of minimal units (i.e., atoms); it was first proposed by an ancient Greek philosopher, Demokritos (ancient Greece, 500 BCE). "Atom" means "unable to be divided." We now know that not only can it be divided, but it can be divided with a massive release of energy, and it's full of other smaller stuff too!

The fundamental subparticles of the atom—electrons, protons, and neutrons—were discovered from experiments carried out during the late nineteenth century and the beginning of the twentieth century.

Even Smaller Pieces of the Puzzle

Physicists Murray Gell-Mann and George Zweig, working separately, each posed the possibility of the quark in 1964. Quarks are fundamental particles that make up everything in the universe. In all, there are six brands of quark, usually paired off and called up/down quarks, charm/strange quarks, and top/bottom quarks. The top quark, though theorized for decades prior, was not discovered until 1995.

There are six types of leptons: electron, electron neutrino, muon, muon neutrino, tau, and tau neutrino.

Thirteen-gauge bosons (force carriers) include the graviton of gravity; the photon of electromagnetism; the W+, W−, and Zen bosons of the weak force; and the eight gluons of the potent force (the reason we have the Relativistic Heavy Ion Collider or RHIC).

Composite subatomic particles (such as protons or atomic nuclei) are bound states of two or more elementary particles. Composite particles include all hadrons (the reason we have a Large Hadron Collider), a group composed of baryons (e.g., protons and neutrons) and mesons (e.g., pions and kaons).

The smallest theoretical particle: An object smaller than a quark has been found, but not directly. This object is the *singularity*, which is theoretically found at the center of every black hole. Each galaxy is theorized to have a black hole at its center. This is a place where all the laws of physics, mathematics, or anything else break down and are cast aside. Our universe, in theory, started with a singularity. Stephen Hawking said that he believes that the Big Bang was two of the multiverses either colliding or splitting.

Is your head spinning yet? It should be, but that was not our intention. Our point in all of this is that some wild stuff has been theorized out there by our own quantum scientists for better than a hundred years at this point. These things could explain how a human being could be abducted and taken through a solid object or how a beam of light could lift someone into a craft or even create invisibility. We are within striking distance of saying, "Ah ha! That's how they do it." Hopefully some of those great minds out there will read this book. We need our ah-ha moment.

Speaking of Great Minds

Michio Kaku is a theoretical physicist. Quantum physicists believe that there really are parallel universes or multiverses. We are energy. Energy travels in waves. Waves vibrate and split apart over time. Steve Weinberg uses the example of a radio in your room tuned to one frequency while the room is actually filled with all the frequencies. When two universes are in phase, they are coherent, and you could move back and forth, but as time starts to evolve, these two universes decouple. They start to vibrate at different frequencies and can no longer interfere with each other. Your radio can only listen to one wave frequency because your radio is de-cohered. It is no longer vibrating in unison with these other frequencies. Fortunately, our technology allows you to turn the dial on the radio and travel from one frequency to the other. Suddenly, a whole new channel with different content emerges from the newly acquired frequency.

Alien technology may have developed to the point of control where the aliens have the capability to manipulate the strong nuclear forces within molecular structure. If they have the capability to change molecular vibration within their craft or on the envelope around their craft, this may explain the invisibility factor. By making the craft de-cohere from our present universe's vibration, this may alter if in fact it is present in our universe or dimension at all!

Hugh Everett III (November 11, 1930–July 19, 1982) was an American physicist who first proposed the many-worlds interpretation (MWI) of quantum physics or multiverse, which he termed his "relative state" formulation. In Everett's formulation, parallel universes may in principal quantum interfere (i.e., "merge" instead of "splitting") with each other. Maybe this is how an alien being travels through a bedroom wall and seems by all senses to be solid and real yet passes through a solid object.

Way-out stuff, we know, but think about how far our technology has come in the last ten years. Where it could be in a thousand years is unfathomable.

Many people have pointed to the scenario that if aliens are coming from some star system light years away, travel time would be impractical by our current knowledge. If these beings are coming from another de-cohered universe or dimension, then this could explain some of the almost magical and incomprehensible reported abilities. Also, it is a common misconception to think that branches of this multiverse are completely separate. By our years of interaction with abductees, there is a very high likelihood that the people having these experiences are gifted mentally, with some extraperceptive abilities. Our findings, as well as those by many other researchers, have seen this trend extend to almost 100 percent of people acknowledging some type of contact with alien beings. Quantum physics suggests that, for example, déjà vu or having premonitions is probably not possible between other parallel universes or multiverse because we should have decoupled or de-cohered from them breaking any connection, but what about within our own? The aliens might be able to tap into this form of communication while cohered within our vibration or phase. This is where quantum entanglement and nonlocality might come into play.

Telepathy may come from quantum entanglement, which is when particles or even large molecules interact physically and then are separated but continue to act as one or in one state, although they may now be separated by great distances. It is suggested that everything was quantum entangled at the moment of the Big Bang and may still be. The theory of quantum entanglement has been around a long time. It was first written about by Albert Einstein in 1935, in a joint paper with Boris Podolsky and Nathan Rosen (Albert Einstein, Boris Podolsky, and Nathan Rosen, "Can Quantum-Mechanical Description of Physical Reality Be Considered Complete?," *Physical Review* 47 [1935]: 777–780). In this study, they formulated the EPR (Einstein, Podolsky, Rosen) paradox. It very basically states that two completely separate quantum systems can and do entangle;

it is like an umbilical cord strung between two objects, and they cohere and vibrate in the same phase on a quantum level. Physicists say that to get two minds to vibrate at the same frequency or phase is probably not possible between universes due to de-coherence, but if this has been overcome by alien technology and quantum interference is possible, then why couldn't an abductee be sent a telepathic message to go outside or go for a drive to a secluded spot to be rendezvoused with a waiting craft. Or for that matter, if an abductee can become quantum entangled by them to be synced with their molecular phase, is this how they take a person through a solid wall, by de-cohering that person with their own universe? Maybe the "buzzing" that abductees report hearing at the onset of the abduction is part of this process that is done to them.

All abductees have enhanced mental attributes of perception. Every person claiming a close encounter or abduction also reported knowing things that they had no idea how they knew—seeing the future, clairvoyance, empathic abilities, or, in some cases, out-of-body experiences.

Do their experiences cause the enhancement of these traits? Or are these traits the reason that they are able to be controlled and taken? It generally follows along family lines; so, does having a genetic ability to bridge that decoupled wavelength or frequency make them susceptible to being controlled?

Maybe abductees can see UFOs and others can't because, in a sense, they (the abductees) have a piece of both worlds and phase sensory ability.

14

CASE FILES FOR MACHINERY DEVICES CONTROLLED

NOT ALL ABDUCTIONS TAKE PLACE IN THE bedroom. Another aspect of the abduction phenomenon is how a person can be abducted when he or she is not in bed asleep and nowhere near the home at all, as seems to be the most common type of abduction. The person may be driving home from work, going to work, on the job, or just driving from here to there. Somehow the UFO occupants know where the subject they want is and how to find them. We've already discussed the possibility that they have a tracking device implanted in their subject, or a mind-reading capability that allows them to find and control the individual. However, we are finding out that the aliens have a method of getting the people they want to be less evasive and more cooperative. They simply do what they do and stop the vehicle like they have someone in the car turning the key off. How do they do that?

If an abduction is brought about by the alien entities controlling a person's mind so that he surrenders his will to resist and is able to be manipulated to believe what he is told and to forget his experience, then how are the vehicles or other devices controlled when the abductee is trying to use one—such as a car, cell phone, or watch?

Too many reports have been submitted where the abductee claims that his or her car suddenly shut off or the cell phone stopped working when the person was trying to use its camera or to call for help. Then, when the episode is over, everything turns back on as if coming back to life—the car is able to turn on or it turns on automatically, the camera and phone work, and the watch is also working.

Investigators Chuck Modin, Vicki Le Blanc, and Richard Lang conducted a MUFON Star Team investigation interview of a UFO witness and possible abductee—a man who was driving home from work after midnight.

Port Jervis, New York:

I left work at 12 a.m., as I work 4 p.m. till 12 a.m.; I work in Unionville, which is approximately fifteen minutes from Port Jervis, where I live; the quickest route is to take the Minisink Turnpike, then to the Greenville Turnpike. I was driving on the Minisink Turnpike when I noticed lights in the sky; firstly I thought it was a plane, then I noticed it had five lights on it from end to end. The lights went from blue-white-red-white-blue in that order, but the strangest thing was it was turning clockwise slowly, and the only sound I could hear was like a cat purring, I slowed the car down to around 20 mph to get a better look, then I noticed the size; it must of been around 200 feet in length. I proceeded to speed up as I started to get nervous, but as it passed over the car, the car turned off without my turning it off, so I came to a stop and grabbed my cell phone and noticed that had turned off too. By this time I didn't know whether to get out of the car and run or stay in my car; before I came to the decision, the lights in the sky had gone out and the car started up. I put my foot down and sped up the road, not looking back. I tell you it was the most unnerving thing to happen to me.

At about 3:50 a.m. on March 20, 1992, patrolman Luis Delgado in Haines City (near Orlando), Florida, was checking the doors at local businesses. After turning onto 30th Street, he saw a green light in his rearview mirror. Seconds later, the interior of his patrol car was illuminated with a green glow. An object began pacing his car, moving from the right side to the front of the vehicle several times. Delgado called police dispatch at 3:52 a.m. and asked for backup, saying, "Something is following the vehicle." When the object moved in front of his car for the third time, Delgado pulled off the road. When he did so, the engine, lights, and radio on his patrol car ceased to function.

The object was about 15 feet long and thin, with a 3-foot-high central area. It was a strange color of green, and the color seemed to "flow over the surface." The object was hovering about 10 feet off the ground. As he was stopped, the object shone a bright white light into the interior of his vehicle. At that point Delgado got out of his car and tried to call police dispatch on his walkie-talkie, but it would not function. He noticed that the air around him had chilled, and he could see his breath fog. According to weather records, the temperature at that time was about 60 degrees Fahrenheit. Shortly thereafter, the object sped away at a fantastic speed in about two or three seconds, moving low over the ground. Another officer arrived just after the object had departed and found Delgado sitting in his police vehicle with the left door open and one foot on the ground. He was shaking and crying and unable to talk. Eventually, he recovered and filed an incident report. The patrol car functioned normally after the event, and Delgado suffered no health problems. Review of the calls to the dispatcher indicated that the duration of the event was in the range two to three minutes.

According to Dr. Mark Rodeghier, the director for the Center for UFO Research, several hypotheses have been advanced to explain these effects:

- The ignition or other electrical system may have been disrupted by high static electric or magnetic fields.
- Ignition of the gas-air mixture may have been affected by ionization of the ambient air.
- Fuel may somehow have been prevented from entering or leaving the carburetor.
- The engine operation may have been disrupted by electric fields induced by an alternating magnetic field, possibly of low frequency.

In the book *UFO Abductions* by D. Scott Rogo (1980), the author states that he has a collection of writings by researchers and investigators in the UFO abduction field. One writer named Bill Faill was an investigative reporter. He wrote an article that was originally published in *Fate Magazine* in January 1977. In his article, he tells of a woman who had contacted him to inquire about reporting a UFO experience she and her husband, Peter, had had. Their experience took place in Rhodesia. It starts in a small town called Umvuma, just south of Salisbury.

Frances and her husband, both professional business people, were driving at about 2:00 a.m. when, after a short time, they noticed a light in the sky. The light was getting closer to them and then kept pace with their car. They then realized that the car's lights started to dim on their own. The light from the object flying above them was bright enough to light up the road, so they weren't too concerned. However, Peter, the driver, soon realized that he could no longer control the car. He realized that the car was speeding much faster than he wanted it to, and applying the brakes did nothing to slow it down. He could not accelerate or brake the car. He also had lost control of the steering, and the car was totally under its own control—or that of someone or something else. The vehicle was maintaining its position on the road and making the bends and turns when needed. He tried not to show any fear to his wife because, although there was no control from him, the car seemed completely safe under its own control.

This lasted for about two hours, and then the driver realized that he had full control of the car again. He also saw that the lighted object that had been flying above them and following them had streaked off over the horizon.

They managed to drive to an all-night service station and checked the car over completely but found nothing wrong. They spent the night at a hotel and then embarked again to continue their trip about 5:30 the next morning. It was still dark when they drove off.

They were driving down the road, and nothing unusual happened to them. A few minutes later, Peter saw two unusual lights in the sky above them. These lights did not seem to be like the ones they saw the previous day, and he had complete control of the car. However, soon he realized that he didn't. Again, the car was not under his control. He could not speed it up, slow it down, or turn the wheel in any way. The car started to speed up to over 100 mph, and he couldn't slow it down. Under normal conditions, the car wouldn't be able to exceed 70 mph. Frances then realized that the road they were on was not the road they should have been on. It was straight, and the sides of the road had brush, swamps, and trees, whereas the road they should have been on was curvy and dry with dips along the way. Peter also noticed that the sounds were strange. The radio was playing silently, but there was no road noise. He felt like it was a dream. It should have also been getting lighter outside with the sun rising, but it was still dark and there was no sun. For the next hour and fifteen minutes, Frances fell asleep, and Peter couldn't remember what had happened. Then, at 7:30 a.m., they realized that they were at the destination they were going to. And the sun was "just there," and they had full control of the car again.

In the book *Situation Red: The UFO Siege* (2016), Leonard Stringfield tells of a military noncommissioned officer who went out to watch a meteor shower. He drove out to a place where he thought he would see many. Having seen none, he decided to return to his car and leave. As he did, he noticed disc-shaped objects moving toward him. He got into his car and drove off. At that point, his car engine stopped, an odd glow engulfed his car, and a numbing, tingling feeling came over him. When the officer reached home, he realized that he was missing about an hour and twenty minutes of time.

On January 8, 1974, a 50-year-old night attendant for the Masonic Home in Springfield, Ohio, was leaving at 3:00 a.m. to go home. He got into his car, and it started without any problems, but as he was driving, the lights on the car suddenly dimmed and the engine went dead. A very bright-lighted object in the sky moved slowly to his car. At 3:15 a.m. the lighted object suddenly shot off into the sky, and his car engine instantly started up. As this was happening, a maintenance man from the Masonic Hall was having a problem with his Motorola pager radio. It was going dead, and then it would start up again. Thinking that the batteries were going dead, he replaced them with new ones, but the problem continued (Stringfield 2016).

Here is a case of vehicle control that is surprisingly different from all the others reported. Normally the reports indicate that the vehicle is a gasoline carburetor engine that is stalled. This report is of a tractor trailer with a diesel engine. The driver of the truck made the report about seven years later, when, for an unknown reason, he was an inmate at a state penitentiary.

The report indicated that in 1968 the driver was driving in Michigan during a heavy January snowstorm. At about 12:15 a.m., the driver pulled over to be able to clear some of the accumulated ice on the windshield wipers. He recalls being blinded by a bright light in the sky. When the light, which lasted only a few seconds, was gone, he was bathed in a pale-green, cone-shaped light beam that encompassed both him and the truck. The snow was falling heavily, but none was falling on the area within the cone of light. The driver stated that he could also feel warmth within the green cone of light. At that point, he lost recollection of what had happened for the next five hours. When he became aware of his surroundings again, he was about 20 feet from the truck, and it was still snowing heavily. There was about 5 to 7 inches of snow all around him, but no footprints or tracks in the snow. As he walked back to his truck, he realized that it had stalled, and the temperature of the engine was about 0 degrees. He said that the engine was a 335 Cummins engine, and it does not stall. Also, when he got back into the truck, he developed a headache and nausea, which persisted for the next few days (Stringfield 2016).

It is reported that a car was driving along a road in July 1974 when the occupants noticed an oval-shaped object traveling alongside their car. They were driving in an open area, and as they came close to some homes the object rose higher in the sky but came close again as they got back into an open-road area. The driver then felt as if the object had taken over the control of the car. The driver had a hard time trying to control the actions of the vehicle and at one point had to struggle to get the car back onto the road as it was nearing the object moving alongside it. When the object disappeared, the driver did manage to regain control. The driver complained that the struggle to regain control had put a strain on his shoulder, and it ached (Stringfield 2016).

On November 4 1975, a car with six passengers was traveling in Ross, Ohio, when they spotted a cylinder-shaped UFO hovering over some trees. They described it as 75 feet in diameter, with blue and green rotating lights. As they watched the object, a small, round ball of red light was ejected from the object. The car's engine and lights suddenly stopped. The red ball of light disappeared, and they noticed the landing gear coming out from the bottom of the object. The landing gear glowed blue light. As soon as the object landed out of sight of the car, into the wooded area, the car's lights and engine started up again. They also noticed that the sound of the insects in the woods could now be heard (Stringfield 2016).

On November 2, 1968, in Villareal de Ebro, Spain, as related in Vicente-Juan Ballester Olmos's book *A Catalogue of 200 Type I UFO Events in Spain and Portugal*, five soldiers were driving in a car when they saw what looked like the sun rising. It was a large, yellow disk rising west of them instead of from the east. As this happened, their car radio, headlights, and engine all shut off on their own as the object landed about 1,640 feet (500 m) from them. They described the object as about the size of an arena. After about three minutes, the object rose and left. Everything that had stopped operated normally again (Ballester Olmos 1976).

Regarding Gasoline Engine Cylinder Mixture Firing upon UFO Leaving Proximity

The fact that a mechanic had an incident of an auto shutdown during a UFO event and concluded that the automatic restart of the vehicle was due to compressed fuel mixture within the cylinder firing, as well as starting the engine upon the reinitiation of the electrical system when the UFO left the proximity, has a few holes in the theory.

1. Piston ring gaps: Each cylinder has a piston with a series of compression and oil-scavenging rings on it to contain compression of the fuel mixture. You need more than just fuel and air to fire an engine; you need compression of that mixture to have an explosion within the cylinder to produce enough power to move the automobile.

Each of the rings in any conventional engine has end gaps in the rings. These end gaps are slight, being on average 0.016 to 0.030 thousandths of an inch, depending on cylinder wear and original bore size. End gaps means that the ring is not a complete circle; it has a slight gap in it to allow the ring to be flexed and installed within the groove made for it in the piston.

Enter mean piston speed. As a piston travels within its cylinder bore, the faster it goes, and the less effect the end gaps have on compression leakage. The compression can leak by that gap of .016 thousandths of an inch only so fast. Past a certain point the piston is compressing the mixture much faster that the leak can occur, resulting in the proper compression buildup to fire the cylinder.

As wear of the cylinders and rings happens over time, compression drops. The end gaps get bigger and the leak down gets faster. This drop results in less power and performance of the engine, until it reaches a point where the engine will not start even though it has fuel and air. It lacks the compression.

Another point in passing on compression rings: They do make gapless piston rings for racing applications that do leak down, and at a very slow rate. All passenger vehicles and commercial vehicles used by the public use rings *with* gaps in them. Only certain racing engines use gapless rings, and then it is a choice of the engine builder. It is not a factor in this case.

Leak down: As an engine stops turning the crankshaft, the pistons stop moving up and down in the cylinders and compression stops being produced. Within a period of seconds, the compression of the cylinder will begin to leak down past the rings into the crankcase. As the compression leaks down, so does the chance of the cylinder being refired, due to lack of compression, an essential part of the explosive process.

Thus, if an automobile electrical system is shut down by a UFO, unless the system is brought back online within a few seconds, compression will leak past the point of no return and will not fire, even if the spark plug were to generate a spark to light the mixture. The system would need the starter engaged to rotate the crankshaft and piston assembly to compress the mixture back to a suitable level to explode the air and fuel mixture. Just turning the power back on is not going to work.

2. Another factor with an engine and the possibility of compression being left in a cylinder is the configuration of the engine, meaning whether it is a four-, six-, or eight-cylinder engine. Four-cycle engines (as opposed to a two-cycle such as an off-road motorcycle or a chain saw) require intake, compression, firing, and exhaust cycles of each cylinder, which requires a crank rotation of two complete turns to complete. A four-cylinder engine has a lesser chance of being in the exact position for a compression fire than an engine with more cylinders. Inline four-cylinders fire at 180 degrees of crank rotation, 90-degree-cylinder banked V-6 engines normally fire at 120 degrees of crank rotation, and V-8s fire at every 90 degrees of crank rotation.

A V-8 would have more of a chance to be in the right crank position to fire a compressed cylinder than a six- or four-cylinder. The more cylinders, the better the chance, but leak down would keep this from happening. Any engine that would sit without running for a couple of minutes to a couple of hours would have all its compression completely leaked off and could not fire even if the spark plug were to light.

3. Relays: Today's cars are loaded with electrical relay switches. A relay switch has at least two circuits in it. One circuit is completed; for example, like turning the ignition switch to energize a small electromagnetic coil to close another set of spring-loaded electrical contacts within the relay to engage the electrical solenoid on the starter motor.

When power is cut to the vehicle, all the spring-loaded relay coils snap back to the open or closed position, whichever is required within that circuit. Relays are used for starters, horns, and many safety features such as ASD (auto shutdown) relays.

ASD relays control the fuel and ignition systems on most all cars and trucks produced with fuel-injected engines in the past thirty years. ASD switches/relays turn off the fuel pump and ignition in case of a collision or turnover of the vehicle. No fuel to pump and feed a potential fire, and no spark to light a fire.

If power to the car is stopped, all the relays would snap back into their normal nonrunning position and would require the turning of the ignition key to crank the engine. The ignition system then feeds a signal to the ASD relay that the engine is being cranked, and allows the startup of the electric fuel pump to produce fuel pressure, so that can be fed to the electronic fuel injectors, which are energized by the computer, which sees a signal from the turning of the crank sensor via the starter switch being turned and the ignition being energized to fire up the sequential energizing of the injectors in relation to the piston intake stroke.

As you see, it is quite complicated these days, and just merely turning the power off and back on without touching anything else such as the turning of the ignition switch makes it highly unlikely that the engine just comes back on without some other unknown process at this point. Occam's razor suggests that the simplest and most logical solution is usually correct. Not the case here.

4. Remote Starters: If a car had a remote starter wired into the system, it would be possible to tap into the frequency of the key fob starter and initiate it, but most cars do not have key starters installed. The latest technology allows people with a smartphone to remotely start their car, but again this is only on the latest off-the-assembly-line cars within the past couple of years. My car is a 2006 GM and has OnStar, which allows the company to track my car and even shut it down by satellite signal if it is stolen, but they can't start it. So, if the UFO tapped into the OnStar signal, the occupants could shut off my car, unlock my doors, and check my emissions, but that is where it ends. No restarting.

At this point, we do not understand the mechanism involved in the spontaneous restarting of an automobile by a UFO. People who have close encounters while on the road and have their car shut down often don't remember the whole encounter, or sometimes only certain points; maybe it is as simple (thank you Occam) as being told not to remember restarting the car themselves with the keys.

Camera Malfunctions

Frank Soriano, coauthor of the book *UFOs Above the Law* (2011), told me (Jim) of two instances in which he has had camera malfunctions while attempting to take pictures of a UFO. Frank has been able to take many photographs and videos of them. Analysis of the object, which seemingly has been stalking him, provides no evidence of an explanation for its identity.

One day, Frank got an urge to go outside with his camera, as he has a few times in the past. As he headed for the door, he checked his camera and everything was fine. There was film in the camera and the batteries were fully charged. When he got out into his driveway, he waited a few minutes and then saw the same peanut-shaped object he has successfully videotaped and photographed before. As he raised the camera and tried to take a picture, the camera would not work. The batteries seemed dead. He missed his chance and went back into the house. As he did, the camera came on and the batteries were fine.

Another time, Frank got the urge to go outside with his camera; he was able to take twelve pictures of the object moving across the sky. Getting the film developed, he discovered something that to this day puzzles him. Frank recalls taking twelve pictures of the object crossing the sky, and eventually losing sight of it behind a tree blocking his view. The object in each picture shows a progressive movement toward that part of the sky. The twelfth picture shows no object as it has gone behind the tree. When he looked at all the pictures, he saw that there were thirteen pictures, and that the thirteenth picture was the one taken of the tree after the UFO had already passed by. Frank is positive he only took twelve pictures, and that the twelfth one became a picture of the UFO having moved back in the progression and is visible with a cloud, which Frank insists was not in the sky at the time. He's not sure how or what happened, but he is convinced that somehow he, his camera, and time have been manipulated.

Aircraft and Electromagnetic Interference Effects

According to Dr. Richard Haines, PhD, at the 1992 MUFON symposium, there have been some considerable studies of vehicles that have had electromagnetic interference (EMI) effects due to nearby UFOs. From what we can find, Dr. Haines is the only one who concentrated on just aircraft and not cars and trucks.

Dr. Haines did his presentation on fifty-six sightings by aircraft pilots in which there was some form of electromagnetic interference. All fifty-six incidents happened only while an unknown object was seen or was nearby the aircraft. There were no problems either before the objects were nearby or after they left. The aircraft varied in size and type. There were private planes such as Piper Cubs or Cessna. The commercial planes were DC-9s, DC-10s, B-737s, B-747s, etc. Military planes were not exempt from this phenomenon, and they were C-46s, C-130s, B-29s, B-36s, F-4s, F15Cs, F-104s, and various others. In Haines's study, there were more military planes involved than all the others combined.

The EMI effects involved interference of ignition systems, radios, radar, lights, power reductions, and/or complete engine shut downs. In one instance of a military plane, the weapons system (sidewinder missile) control panel ceased to function. In nine of the cases, reciprocating engines either stalled or completely shut down.

It appears that the UFOs not only caused havoc with all the equipment listed above, but they also caused a great deal of worldwide concern for the human race in what might have led to the destruction of property and loss of life.

Early in the morning of March 16, 1967, a series of lights were spotted above the area of the Malmstrom Air Force Base, Montana, which is the site for intercontinental ballistic missiles (ICBMs). The two witnesses were air force security policemen and members of the Security Alert Team. They were patrolling the grounds when they saw the lights doing acrobatic maneuvers above them. When the lights got bigger and closer to the base, they called Robert Salas, who at the time was on duty as the deputy missile combat crew commander for Oscar Flight LCF (Launch Control Facility). Salas asked them to describe what they were seeing.

Salas did not display much concern over the sighting and told them to call back if the lights get any closer. Soon after, one of the men did call back, and the urgent sound in his voice caused Salas to be a little more concerned. Salas this time went and woke up his commander to brief him on what was happening. In the middle of the briefing and before Salas could give all the information, alarms started going off. A "no go" light indicating a problem at one of the missile sites went on. Almost immediately there was another light indicating a problem at another site, and then two more. Soon there were ten lights indicating that the missiles were shutting down without cause.

As the two men were trying to determine what had happened to cause the shutdown, they learned that the same thing had happed at the Echo Flight LCF, where ten other ICBMs had shut down.

There were now about twenty missiles shut down for no apparent reason. There were no reports of power being lost at either site. Each missile had gone off-line due to a fault in the guidance and control system. At both sites there were reports of UFOs near the base. The missiles remained out of service for an entire day until maintenance crews were able to put them back into service (Robert Salas and James Klotz, *Faded Giant*, 2005).

On October 4, 1982, in the winding-down years of the Cold War, a few unidentified lights were seen performing acrobatics in the sky near Usovol, Ukraine, as reported by some military officials around 7:30 to 9:37 p.m. near a Russian military missile base.

The Ukraine was still a part of the USSR at this time. The sighting of the UFOs wasn't too big of a concern for the officials at the base, but the effects they caused were. Whereas in 1967 at the Malmstrom Missile Base in Montana, the missiles were turned off, the missiles at Usovol were activated for launch.

"For a short time, signal lights on both control panels suddenly turned on, the lights showing that missiles were preparing for launching. This should only happen if an order was transmitted from Moscow," according to Air Force colonel Boris Sookolov (ret.), who was in charge of the investigation of the incident. No reason for the activation of the launching could be determined, and had the missiles launched it might have led to war with Russia, possibly World War III.

Tests of the system indicated that the panels were operating normally before and after the incident. Who or what activated the control panels to launch the codes to the missiles was not determined or at least was not reported (www.openminds.tv/soviet-nukes-and-ufos/).

Another incident involving UFOs and a nuclear problem happened on July 24, 1984, in Westchester County, New York, at the Indian Point Nuclear Reactor Complex, which lies along the Hudson River in the town of Buchannan.

On this date, a UFO was spotted by eleven security guards at the plant. Most of the guards there were former NYC police officers, and some of these officers were witnesses. What they saw was a giant UFO hovering over one of the reactors at the plant. A few witnesses in Peekskill, New York, a nearby town, had seen the UFO over the nuclear plant as well.

Only one of the three reactors was in operation at the time, and that was the one the UFO decided to hover above. As it approached the reactor, the security system shut down. The alarm system would not work. Inside the security consoles, the computers that control all the security and communications shut down. However, and fortunately, the reactor did not shut down. Maybe it was because the UFO did not stick around too long. The commander of the plant had requested an Air National Guard helicopter to fly to the plant and shoot the UFO down. It did not hang around long enough for that to happen (Hynek et al. 1998).

15

REGAINING CONTROL

IS IT ALL HOPELESS AND ARE WE condemned to doing the will of these alien abductors, or are there ways we can overcome and prevail? To live our lives as we want to live them, free from fear of losing control and submitting to the will of others—especially alien will.

There are some who feel that it is perfectly okay to submit themselves to the abductors because they believe that the aliens are here to better our world and their lives. There are those who believe that they are being taken against their will and being tortured and forced to do things they do not want to do. We say, if they want to live with the abductions, then go ahead. For those others who are tired of the intrusions, we hope to help with ways to end them.

A few abductees will get to a point in their experience where if they feel they can exert some type of control over their experience, they can somehow make it through it.

If the average person is placed into a situation where they perceive themselves as having no control, suddenly it is a very uncomfortable place. Most of us require a certain amount of control within our lives to feel safe and secure. As an adult you have control over where you live, how you live, what you do for work, and the control and guidance of your children—or you may have a profession that is based on control, such as the military or law enforcement, where strict control is the norm.

A position of control is often attractive to certain personality types. It is a good feeling to be in control, right? Type A personalities, especially with

OCD (obsessive compulsive disorder), are often drawn to a position of power and control because that is the only place or position that they feel safe. People of this personality type and profession may have a much-rougher time adjusting to the abduction experience.

In her book *How To Defend Yourself against Alien Abduction* (1998), Ann Druffel gives nine methods that have been tried and proven to defend oneself against alien abductions. We can't promise that all of these will work all the time, but they have worked for the abductees noted in Ann's book. Some of these methods have been tried by some of the abductees we have told you about earlier in the chapter.

- Mental struggle: Block their mind control.
- Physical struggle: Fight back.
- Righteous anger: Summon your individual rights.
- Protective rage: Guard your loved ones.
- Support from family members
- Intuition: Sense them coming.
- Metaphysical methods: Create a personal shield.
- Appeal to personal personages: Get help from on high.
- Repellents: Use time-tested fend-off substances.

There have been reports that some abductees have managed to terminate an abduction by trying to fight back. Physically fighting back seems almost impossible; however, some reports claimed that by building up enough intense anger and inner strength, an abduction can be stopped by yelling at the aliens. Some have claimed that by yelling to God or Jesus or praying (the website AlienResistence.org displays hundreds of testimonies of this), they have been able to get the aliens to release their control. Others claim that just yelling at them to stop and get away has worked. We're not saying these will work every time, and probably not as often as they have failed, but almost anything you do to discourage them or make it feel like it's not worth the effort could cause the abduction to possibly be terminated.

Some people who have been abducted numerous times and have wanted to end it have tried other things. Some have had themselves (with the help of others) tied to the bed or strapped down to make their removal difficult. One person reported leaving marbles on the floor to make it difficult for entry into the room.

I Tripped One of Them

A number of years ago, I had a fellow who I (Bob) worked with for a while who I believed was a genuine abductee. John (pseudonym) contacted me all excited because he had managed to have a small inkling of control over the entities during the previous night's abduction. He had been aware of his experiences for some time. He knew when they were going to be coming for him, he knew how they entered his house, and he knew how they moved around. He had or was allowed to be conscious enough to get a feel for how it was done and to see patterns involved in his taking.

His bedroom was located at the end of a hallway in his home, and the entities would come walking down the hall, usually a group of three small Greys, enter his bedroom, and initiate his abduction, which included taking him down the hallway to his bathroom, out through the solid wall of the shower stall, and up a beam of light to a waiting craft.

John had gotten the feeling, as most longtime experiencers do, that this night they would be coming for him. Anxiety started to set in, and waiting for it to happen became the focus of the rest of the time beforehand. John had gotten upset with the total lack of regard they had shown him, and wanted a little payback. So he put a small plan in motion.

Knowing that they always come down the hallway, John strung a trip wire very low in the doorway to the bedroom. Fearing that they would somehow read his mind and know about it, he tried his best to block it from his thoughts to hide it from them.

Soon evening fell. John focused the best he could on other things and waited. The feeling of them coming became more pronounced. The low vibrational hum could be felt by John; he knew it would not be long. He had propped himself up on his pillows to be able to see the doorway to the bedroom, which he always left open since he lived alone. Suddenly, he found himself frozen. Unable to move. A chilling but now common sense that he knew well. John sensed movement in the hall and could see shadows. Three short Greys could be seen preparing to enter his bedroom from the hallway. John was so scared that he had forgotten all about the trip wire he had installed earlier. The first Grey entered the doorway and caught the trip wire, tumbling face first to the floor! The other two suddenly stopped as if in shock, gazing at the first on the floor and then at John. He got a sudden rush of feelings from them as if they were stunned by his ability to do this to them, as well as a strong feeling of disapproval.

John was no longer scared. He was elated. He had made an effort to create a cause and effect within his experience and was successful. He had done something to them. His will had triumphed in changing the experience. He had become unpredictable to them. Their control on him from that day forth seemed lessened to him; although he continued to have abductions, he always from that time forth got the feeling from them that "we need to be on our toes around you."

John gained a small amount of control that day. It wasn't much, but it was enough. He knew they could be tricked and weren't infallible. They were now not 100 percent in control of him. Last I heard from John, he was devising new ways to get under their skin. Let the games begin.

Michael Menkin is a retired Federal Aviation Administration technical writer and editor from Kentucky. He is the inventor of a helmet that he claims can and has stopped mind thoughts from the aliens and thus has been able to prevent abductions. On his website (www.stopabductions.com) he claims that the thought screen helmet scrambles telepathic communication between aliens and humans. Aliens cannot immobilize people wearing thought screens, nor can they control their minds or communicate with them by using their telepathy. When aliens can't communicate to control humans, they do not take them. He says it is a simple helmet to make, and he will send directions, for free, to anyone who wishes to make one.

16

CONCLUSION

QUESTIONS, QUESTIONS, AND MORE QUESTIONS . . .

Are we being visited? Are we being taken? Do we have a choice? Can we do anything about it?

And this is only a part of the mess we've gotten ourselves into. Yes, we did say "we've gotten ourselves into." There are several things we could have done about this whole abduction problem.

One is to be informed. Have we done enough to know what is going on, or are we hiding our heads in the sand, hoping it will all go away? And when we do learn about it, what are we doing about it? *Not much*, you say? You may be right, and that may be the start to turn this all around. Knowledge gives us the power to arm ourselves. Knowledge makes us responsible for all that goes on. We can no longer hide. We need to get our heads out of the sand and look around. Knowledge of what is happening gives us a chance to plan, to set in motion our defenses. Knowledge should make us want to tell others about what is happening. To stand up on the highest mountains and shout to the world that we are under attack and we need to fight back. Maybe not all of us are the ones being abducted, but it is happening, and we most likely know someone who it is happening to. How can we help them if we don't help ourselves?

Is our government or military going to do anything for us? As far as they are concerned, the problem doesn't exist. We are just fanatics who are fantasy prone and conspiracy crazy. Since 1947, when a UFO "allegedly" crashed in Roswell, New Mexico, the military has lied, slandered, and threatened people who claim to be witnesses to some aspect of the incident that the military says didn't happen.

Can we really believe that they don't know anything that has happened, not just in Roswell but in any place in our country? The world? With all the satellites, radar, and cameras, can we really believe that if this is really happening and we are not really crazy that they aren't aware? It has been said that they have documented every single piece of scrap, garbage, nut, bolt, and any other object floating in our space outside our atmosphere. If a small piece of satellite falls from space, they know where it is going to land almost even before it gets there. The North American Aerospace Defense Command (NORAD) is a US and Canadian binational organization charged with the missions of aerospace warning and aerospace control for North America. Aerospace warning includes the monitoring of man-made objects in space, and the detection, validation, and warning of attack against North America, whether by aircraft, missiles, or space vehicles, through mutual support arrangements with other commands (www.norad.mil/about/index.html). Yes, that did say space vehicles, and we are sure it didn't just reference satellites. So, with all the technology that there is, how can we believe that they don't know what we know? Since they can't explain it, they have to deny it. It doesn't exist. It therefore is classified with other folklore and conspiracy theories, such as the Loch Ness Monster, Bigfoot, and ghosts, for instance.

So, what other explanation can we come up with?

Is the Government in Cahoots with Aliens?

What part does our government and military have in all of this? There is definitely enough proof and information throughout the many published materials on and off the World Wide Web to remove any doubt that they have been affiliated in some form or other in the abduction of its own people and that of ordinary citizens. Besides the use of hypnosis, torture, drugs, and other mind games that they have used, the military is probably even to this day still practicing their art in mind control. Imagine how scary it will be if they've succeeded. We may never know—which by itself may be proof. There was a television show shown in the spring season of 2012 on ABC called *Castle*. On one episode they had the killer dressed as a zombie who killed a targeted person. As it turned out, the killer was under the control of another who used a drug called scopolamine. This is a drug normally used for mild suppression of nausea and motion sickness. In this episode, it was used in a heavy-enough dose to put the recipient in a zombie-like trance and as a mind control weapon. He was able to do someone else's bidding no matter how horrible the deed was. A search on the internet gave the description of the drug and its uses, including adverse uses, which also mentioned that it was reported to be one of the drugs used by MKULTRA.

What would benefit the government or the military to go to such lengths to control its own people? Using available subjects mostly without permission, they could study the subject and improve their techniques. But why not use prisoners? Could it be that by using prisoners, who are well guarded, the military would tip off their objective and have to deal with a revolting public, which would put a lot of pressure on an in-office administration and cause all kinds of political fallout? Why wouldn't they just pay people to volunteer; there must be hundreds of people who might need money badly enough to subject themselves to such torture and possibly death? No, they probably figure that what you don't know won't hurt you, and if it does, they can clean up the mess or possibly have it overlooked completely, thus allowing them to continue as they were.

So, what can we do about stopping this from continuing or to begin all over again? It would be hard to get any government agency, or even Congress, to look deeply enough into it since the cost would be so prohibitive, not to mention the time in courts dragging this out. But shouldn't we know that this is going on? After all, knowing is a weapon of defense that could benefit everyone. It might even explain a lot of missing people or mysterious deaths. Now, can we expect to believe that the government is doing all this alone, or are the aliens doing it all, or can they be doing it together?

If the government, or just the military, is in cahoots with aliens, then why? Are they traitors to the American people and the human race? Or are they mercenaries and getting something in return for their services? Something like thirty pieces of silver? Is our government getting technological advancements for their blind eye? What are the aliens getting . . . maybe that blind eye? Allowance to travel anywhere they want and to be able to mutilate animals for whatever reason they have . . . or maybe to abduct people for whatever reason they want? Would our government even be able to stop them if they wanted to, and if not, then why would the aliens make such a deal? It should be obvious that they are not here for our benefit. They may be far more advanced than we are, but they have not offered any medical breakthroughs to save us from the many diseases we have, or pointed out any ideas to better life and improve our economy or live in peace. We *have* come a long way in science technology though. In such a short time we have been able to send men to the moon. We have sent space ships into the far reaches of space. We can communicate with almost anybody, anywhere on the planet, without the use of a landline phone. We can take pictures and send them to ourselves or someone else. We can watch movies or see who we are talking to on our small phones that we carry in our pockets.

Have we benefited from them? The government won't tell us because then they would have to admit that the aliens and UFOs do exist and that they have lied to us for so many years.

It has been rumored that there is an "Inner Government" funded by a "Black Budget," which is doing some underhanded dealings either with or against aliens, either for their own benefit or for a New World Order that may partner with the aliens. Or it might be just to gain what they can and then turn against them also. This sounds like a lot of ifs, ands, or buts, but that is what makes a good conspiracy.

Whether or not the government is complicit with the aliens, we are being visited and we are being used, and, if anybody is being taken willfully, then why? Why would you subject yourself to that kind of abuse? A lot of abductees come back and when they realize that they had been taken, whether consciously or by the assistance of someone else, they tell of all the wonderful things that the aliens can do for us. Or they tell of the warnings they got of impending doom, such as how the world is going to be destroyed by our own hands or by some other means we have no control over. But do they tell anybody when this will happen? Do they tell us how they know this or what can be done about it, or do they offer to help us? It seems they just want to tell us what they think we want to hear.

The lengths that they will go to to make us think that they are not who they really are is another way to show that they have mastered the art of deception. They have been able to make us think that they are someone else. Many reports have come in about someone having seen an owl in places where owls have never been seen before. Or they may appear as another type of animal. One woman reported seeing her dead grandfather walk into her bedroom at night just prior to being abducted. The use of hypnosis or some other mind-controlling method makes abductees think that everything is going to be all right, and that there is no reason to fear—such as how Antonio Villas Boas was able to think that a blond woman who barked during sex was really what she appeared to be.

They've proven that there is no way of hiding from them either. They followed Whitley Strieber from his hometown in Texas to his home in New York City and then to his camp up in the Catskill Mountains. They followed Frank Soriano from his home in Yonkers, New York, to his home in Ticonderoga to his home in Wilton. They followed Anna Jamerson from her home in England to her home in Michigan to her home in Pennsylvania. There are hundreds more examples of people moving and not being able to get away from these aliens.

Are they using implants to keep track of the locations of their subjects? Do they have some kind of—to use a term from the old *Star Trek* shows—a mind meld to keep tabs on abductees? It has been proven by reports from so many different abductees that there is little means of hiding from them. And even with all the contact that abductees are having with their abductors, there is so little we still know about them. What they tell abductees, when they tell them anything, cannot be trusted. It has been proven so many times that they have lied. All they really seem to want is to make people comfortable enough that they don't resist to a point they can't control, so we don't really know why they are doing what they are doing; we can only speculate.

Regardless of why they are doing what they are doing, they are doing it. They are abducting people, and they believe that there is little or nothing we can do about it. We've already learned in an earlier chapter that there is something we can do about it. We can stop them with knowledge. Knowing what to do can put a little more advantage into our hands. First you must decide if you really want to know. If you don't know that you are an abductee but suspect so, you can do things to find out, but once you open the door to that knowledge, it will be too late to close the door and shut out what you learn. However, after you do open the door and learn what has been happening, you can develop strategies to fight back. As in the chapter on how to stop an abduction, you can let them know that you are not going so easily.

Maybe it means putting a trip wire across your bedroom doorway. Or maybe struggling a little harder to yell at them or just trying to move a finger to gain some kind of self-control, you can become something more than a robot following remote controls.

Whatever you choose in your way of resisting, they will somehow overcome these techniques. One note to consider about tying yourself down, as mentioned earlier: if they can take you through a wall or window to remove you from the house, they can take you out from under the ropes. No matter what kind of bedroom tricks you try, remember that not all abductions are done at night. Many are done during the middle of the day. It doesn't even matter if you are in a crowd or not.

You need to build up your self-confidence and be determined that you aren't going to stand for this anymore. If there are some ways that we can discourage these private invasions and attacks on us, we need to learn what they are. Whatever techniques you use, once they stop working, find another. Become annoying to them so they get tired of the frustrations. We need to band together and fight back. There are many support groups throughout this country that are working to help abductees. But be careful; just because someone says they are there to help abductees doesn't mean that they are qualified to do so. Like any other opportunity, some people may be charlatans and out for themselves. Check out any group first. Ask for references; if they are serious about their claims, they will do what they can and still be able to maintain confidentiality. One group that is qualified is ICAR—International Community for Alien Research. This group has directors and support groups throughout the country and is not to be confused with another group that goes by the same acronym of ICAR—International Center of Abduction Research. This second group is headed by David Jacobs, who is a retired professor at Temple University. Jacobs has written many books on the subject of alien abductions and is one of the foremost authorities on the subject. This group, however, is geared more toward the researcher and therapist. Both groups are highly qualified and very reliable for help in dealing with alien abductions. Another group, and one that has been sponsored by the Mutual UFO Network (MUFON), is OPUS (Organization for Paranormal Understanding and Support). The mission of OPUS is to develop a network of people dedicated to a better understanding of the overall nature of unusual/anomalous personal experiences and to support those who have them. Such experiences may include extraordinary states of consciousness; fortean, spiritual, or parapsychological phenomena; close encounters with nonhuman entities; and UFO activity. OPUS, through its educational services and position of neutrality, provides a meeting ground for people and groups of opposing and often-controversial views in the hope that in working together we can further our overall knowledge in these areas and promote scientific research, with the ultimate goal of helping humankind. To that end, OPUS networks with many like-minded organizations, such as John Mack Institute (JEMI), Budd Hopkins and the Intruders Foundation, Dr. Leo Sprinkle and ACCET (Academy of Clinical Close Encounters Therapists Inc.), Yvonne Smith and CERO (Close Encounter Research Organization), and Dr. David Jacobs and ICAR. One of the many ways that OPUS can assist is to offer support to individuals and groups.

Where does all this lead us? Should we listen to those who would mock us and keep our heads in the sand and hope it will all go away, or should we do something about it? We are under attack, and to some extent this is a war. This is technically a universal war. Unless we can prove that there is an interdimensional portal that opens and closes between us and extraterrestrial beings at their will, this is a battle.

President Ronald Reagan brought the possibility of an intergalactic war to the Russians and the United Nations when he set out to build a "Star Wars" weapon in space. Maybe that was an excuse to threaten Russia, but it can and should be used by our government to ward off the aliens and keep us safe. We'd do it with other weapons if we knew we were under attack by another nation, so why not with other life forms such as extraterrestrials? How long before the movie *Independence Day* becomes a reality?

How effective would our weaponry be, though, if they have the ability to control us? Rumors have it that we have been able to shoot down some UFOs, and we have captured some crashed saucers, but what have we learned from them? We would have to assume that we have learned a lot, but in reference to "we," we don't mean "we" the public, but "we" the military and our government.

Don't be a victim, and don't be a pawn. Stand up and resist. And remember that we do not have to stand alone.

Alien Contact Could Be Risky. Discovery Channel, with Stephen Hawking, 2010.

Alternative Considerations of Jonestown & Peoples Temple. https://Jonestown. sdsu.edu.

American Psychiatric Association. *Diagnostic and Statistical Manual of Mental Disorders: DSM-IV*. Washington, DC: American Psychiatric Association, 1994.

Baddeley, Alan, Michael W. Eysenck, and Michael C. Anderson. "Memory. Motivated Forgetting." New York: Psychology Press, 2009.

Baines, C. (Ed. and Trans). *The Writings of Anna Freud (Vol. 2)*. New York: International Universities Press. (Original work published 1936) Freud, S. (1955).

Ballester Olmos, Vicente-Juan. *A Catalogue of 200 Type I UFO Events in Spain and Portugal*. Center for UFO Studies, 1976.

Browning, Robert. *The Pied Piper of Hamelin*. Alcester, UK: Pook, 2017.

Bullard, Thomas E. *UFO Abductions: The Measure of a Mystery*. Vol. 1, *Comparative Study of Abduction Reports*. Bloomington, IN: Fund for UFO Research, 1987.

Collins English Dictionary. Glasgow: HarperCollins, 1979.

Currie, Janice. "Decades later two men find they can discuss strange UFO experience they shared as teens." *UFO Journal* 518 (June 2011).

"December 18, 1926: Gilbert Lewis Coins 'Photon' in Letter to Nature." This Month in Physics History. *APS News* 21, no. 11 (December 2012).

Dispenza, Joe. *Evolve Your Brain: The Science of Changing Your Mind*. Deerfield Beach, FL: Health Communications, 2007.

Dolan, Richard M. *UFOs and the National Security State: The Cover-Up Exposed, 1973–1991*. Rochester, NY: Keyhole, 2010.

Druffel, Ann. *How to Defend Yourself against Alien Abduction*. New York: Three Rivers, 1998.

Einstein, Albert. "On the Generalized Theory of Gravitation." *Scientific American* 182, no. 4 (1950): 13–17.

Lieberman, Robert, dir. *Fire in the Sky*. Written by Tracy Tormé. Based on the book by Travis Walton. DVD. Burbank, CA: Warner Home Video, 1993.

Fowler, Ray. *The Andreasson Affair*. New York: Prentice Hall, 1979.

Fowler, Raymond. *The Allagash Abduction: Undeniable Evidence of Alien Intervention*. Tigard, OR: Wild Flower, 1993.

Freud, Anna. *The Ego and the Mechanisms of Defense*. Translated by Cecil Baines. New York: International Universities Press, 1946.

Fuller, John G. *The Interrupted Journey: Two Lost Hours "Aboard a Flying Saucer."* New York: Dial, 1966.

Heaven's Gate. www.britannica.com/topic/Heavens-Gate-religious-group.

Hendry, Allan. *The UFO Handbook: A Guide to Investigating, Evaluating, and Reporting UFO Sightings*. New York: Doubleday, 1979.

Hopkins, Budd, and Carol Rainey. *Sight Unseen*. New York: Atria Books, 2003.

Howard, Pierce J. *The Owner's Manual for the Brain: Everyday Applications from Mind-Brain Research*. 3rd ed. Austin, TX: Bard, 2006.

http://web.mit.edu/newsoffice/2010.

Hynek, J. Allen, Phillip Imbrogno, and Bob Pratt. *Night Siege: The Hudson Valley UFO Sightings*. New York: Ballentine Books, 1987.

Imbrogno, Phillip. *Ultraterrestrial Contact*. Woodbury, MN: Llewellyn, 2010.

Irving, Washington. *Rip Van Winkle*. London: Penguin Classics, 2016.

Jacobs, David M. *Walking among Us: The Alien Plan to Control Humanity*. San Francisco: Disinformation Books, 2015.

Johnson, Jeffery. "Forgotten Memories Are Still in Your Brain." *Neuron* Magazine, http://www.wired.com/2009/09/forgotten.

Klien, Christopher. "Stockholm Syndrome: The True Story of Hostages Loyal to Their Captor." www.history.com/news/stockholm-syndrome.

Lammer, Helmut, and Marion Lammer. *MILABS: Military Mind Control and Alien Abductions*. Lilburn, GA: IllumiNet, 2000.

Leir, Roger. *Casebook: Alien Implants*. Whitley Strieber's Hidden Agendas Books. New York: Bantam Dell, 2000.

Leong, Stephanie, Wendi Waits, and Carroll Diebold. "Dissociative Amnesia and DSM-IV-TR Cluster C Personality Traits." *Psychiatry (Edgmont)* 3, no. 1 (2006): 51–55.

Markus, Gregory B. "Stability and Change in Political Attitudes: Observed, Recalled, and 'Explained.'" *Political Behavior* 8, no. 1 (1986): 21–44.

McGaugh, James. *Memory and Emotion: The Making of Lasting Memories*. New York: Columbia University Press, 2003.

Mork and Mindy. ABC television network, 1974–1982.

Mottola, Greg, dir. *Paul*. Written by Simon Pegg and Nick Frost. DVD. Universal City, CA: Universal, 2011.

My Favorite Martian. CBS television network, 1963–1966.

Paul Winchell: Biography. http://paulwinchell.net/bio.html.

Pinker, Steven. *How the Mind Works*. New York: W. W. Norton, 1997 (reissued 2009).

Reber, Paul. "What Is the Memory Capacity of the Human Brain?" *Scientific American Mind* 21, no. 2 (May 2010): 70.

Rogo, D. Scott. *UFO Abductions: True Cases of Alien Kidnappings*. New York: Signet Books, 1980.

Schacter, Daniel L. *The Seven Sins of Memory: How the Mind Forgets and Remembers*. Boston: Houghton Mifflin, 2001.

Scott, Ridley, dir. *Alien*. Written by Dan O'Bannon. 1979. DVD. Beverly Hills, CA: Twentieth Century Fox Home Entertainment, 2017.

Shea, James H., ed. *Journal of Geological Education* 30, no. 1 (1982).

SLAC National Accelerator Laboratory. 2575 Sand Hill Road, Menlo Park, CA 94025.

Spencer, John. *The UFO Encyclopedia*. New York: Avon, 1993.

Spielberg Stephen, dir. *Taken*. Sci Fi Channel miniseries, 2002.

Stevens, Henry. *Hitler's Flying Saucers: A Guide to German Flying Discs of the Second World War*. Kempton, IL: Adventures Unlimited, 2003.

Strieber, Whitley. *Communion*. New York: Beech Tree Books, 1987.

Stringfield, Leonard. *Situation Red: The UFO Siege*. New York: Doubleday, 2016.

Sun Tzu. *The Art of War* [ca. 500 BCE]. Translated by Ralph D. Sawyer. Boulder, CO: Westview, 1994.

"Untertassen Sie fliegen aberdoch." *Der Spiegel*, March 30, 1959. Article about and interview of Rudolf Schriever.

Wilson, Kay. MILABS: Project Open Mind (personal papers). DailyDDoSe, 2018. https://dailyddose.wordpress.com/2012/02/21/milabs-project-open-mind-milabs-military-abductions/.

Wise, Robert, dir. *The Day the Earth Stood Still*. 1951. DVD. Beverly Hills, CA: Twentieth Century Fox Home Entertainment, 2008.

Turner, Karla. *Taken: Inside the Alien-Human Abduction Agenda*. CreateSpace, 2013.

Turner, Karla. *Into The Fringe: A True Story of Alien Abduction*. Berkeley, CA: Berkeley Books, 1992.

www.bibliocapleyades.net/ufoaleman/rfz/chapter3a.htm J. Andreas Epps

www.history.com/topics/us-government/history/-of'-mkultra

IN MEMORIAM

STANTON FRIEDMAN
(JULY 1934-MAY 2019)

We would like to take a moment to remember Stanton Friedman, a well-known nuclear physicist and professional ufologist, who has done so much to advance the research, investigation, and the knowledge of UFO phenomena—bringing all of it to the mainstream from the outer fringe. His books inspired others to take a closer look at UFOs and his investigation of the UFO crash at Roswell, which is now legendary.

We will miss him, his warm smile, and his cutting wit. Thank you, Stan. May God bless you and may you RIP.